SUGAR AND SPICE AND EVERYTHING THAT'S NOT SO NICE

A Serial Entrepreneur's Journey of Start-ups!

SUGAR AND SPICE AND EVERYTHING THAT'S NOT SO NICE

A Serial Entrepreneur's Journey of Start-ups!

G. Ramachandran

Ocean Books Pvt. Ltd.

Published by
Ocean Books (P) Ltd.
4/19 Asaf Ali Road,
New Delhi-110 002 (INDIA)
e-mail: info@oceanbooks.in

ISBN 978-81-8430-641-5
SUGAR AND SPICE AND EVERYTHING THAT'S NOT SO NICE
by G. Ramachandran
Edited by: Dr. Shabnam Asthana

Edition
First, 2022

Price
₹ 300.00 (Rupees Three Hundred only)

Printed at

Nakshatra Art, New Delhi

I dedicate this book to my rock-solid support system and lifelines:

My wife Priya Ramachandran who has been the calming and reassuring influence in my life giving me wings and wisdom whenever needed.

and

My loving daughter Roopa Ramachandran- my lifeline, whose smiling innocent self has always helped me find the light through the toughest of times.

Without you, Priya and Roopa, I could never have pursued this start up journey and will remain forever indebted to you both for your unconditional love and support all through my career.

My appreciation for two outstanding team members-

- Rahul Jain
- Tanujit Brahma

Author's Note

For those who say success breeds contentment I may be the anomaly that just got added to their list of discoveries.

Plush corporate corridors, expensive suits, jet setting across the world in five-star comfort and luxury, I had it all. But had I reached my destination, was the question that plagued me then. If this was what people aspired for, why was I not engulfed with happiness,elation and the desire to rest on my laurels?

While people regaled in the word success and all that it entailed, life for me proved to be a bundle of contradictions. It gave me a harsh jolt when I was at the very pinnacle of success, leaving me vulnerable and reactive.

What was it about success that lashed out at me and shook me and never allowed me to rest on my complacency? I could sense a high degree of restlessness, and a deep craving to give it all up. This recklessness was not looking for an anchor in the mountains and sainthood, albeit that had its own charm, but that was not what I had in mind then. The gnawing feeling that I was consumed with, compelled me to give up everything and start my corporate success story from scratch. Somewhere down the line, the fascination of a regular job and working for others had lost its charm. I wanted to venture into what would be MY enterprise.

So was I the starry eyed individual who believed that a leader in the corporate world had the pre requisite and stamp of success to make his mark in the start-up world? In hindsight, probably yes, as part of the bravado stemmed from that. The rest, I must admit was passion and the confidence to branch off on my own. The excitement of jumping headlong into the vast sea of possibilities that was beckoning me, to launch my own voyage of discovery and success, made me heady with exuberance.

The birth of an idea can be both extremely invigorating and incredibly risky, more so, when it involves embarking on a start-up. At the beginning of your voyage you are like a rudderless ship steered by the winds of your passion and where being “at sea” assumes a poignant, realistic proportion.

The picture of the choppy sea and the wind lashing at the stern of the ship was not out of a novel that I was reading, as I soon realized. I could feel the cold damp air and the uncertainty of the next wave that would hit the ship I was sailing in. ***Yes it was my story and it was my journey.***

Did I say my? No, let me correct myself here, for it could be the journey of most of you who are intrigued by the idea of start-ups. Through my experiences I aim to unveil this mystic world. A world that has often been talked about and interpreted in manifold ways. I will delineate the risks and advantages. Interestingly here, mine will be triple the risk or triple the advantage since I had decided to shed the number ***one*** starting with my position in the corporate world. I had succumbed to the lure of the number 3 and that was the count of the number of start-ups I began with! My fascination with numbers kept growing; as I went on to establish a total of ***15*** start-ups.

During my adventure packed journey, I was knocked down, lifted up, flung to the nadir, catapulted to success, yes I have seen and braved it all. The lens of my start-up vision is now crystal clear and my observations in this book practical and realistic. I have interspersed my narrative with anecdotes, and real life situations.

If you are a start-up enthusiast, my entrepreneurial journey will be that beacon of light that shows you the road ahead. The topography is a challenging one. It is dotted with twists and turns, highs and lows but incredibly satisfying. My journey will be the precursor to arm you with a solid road map for converting your start-up dream to successful reality!

If you believe that every start-up has to traverse the road from zero to hundred then this book will serve as your guide to get you there!

As for me "am I a successful failure? With success in success and success in failure, with a unique success failure travel map?"

I leave it to you to judge me and my serial entrepreneurial journey.

Read on and live my experiences as I foray into the start- up world and its clichéd universe to discover my own significant meanings through my successes and failures!

Contents

Author's Note 7

1. Close Encounters of the Oxymoronic Kinds! 13
2. Turbulence–Ideas and the Situational Conflict! 19
3. Liberty Laced With Responsibility! 27
4. Setting Sail-Donning Multihued Caps-Deck Hand to Captain! 34
5. The Start-up Coexistence – Success and Debacle! 42
6. Fitting the People Pieces in the Start-up Jigsaw Puzzle 49
7. Sowing Ideas for Success in the Fertile Start-up Ground, Paying Heed to the Seasons 56
8. Choosing People Wisely–Those Who Fan the Embers of the Start-up Fire Instead of Dousing Its' Flames! 63
9. Reinventing People Dynamics and Seasoning It With Experience! 70
10. The Go-to-market Strategy–the Nerve Center of All Start-ups! 78

11. The Start-up Misnomer– Awards vs Rewards 86
12. A Start-up Essential– Desperation to Conviction!............. 94
13. Partnerships in Start-ups– Enriching or Inhibiting?........ 103
14. Start-up Failures Are Inevitable but so Is Learning! 111
15. Options, Decisions and Reflections............. 120
16. Trading My Shiny Corporate Shoes for a Pair of Sneakers–Sprint Ready on New Turf! 128
17. Reflections on the Method in My Madness.................... 136
18. Rummaging Through the Hat of Experience and Pulling Out the Critical Success Factors for Start-ups. ... 144
19. Fixing the Remaining Pieces of the Start-up Puzzle to Complete the Picture!.. 152
20. Hanging Up My Boots or Moving on? Coupling the Past With a Compelling Vision for the Future................ 159
21. Vantage Point–A Bird's Eye View! 163
22. On and beyond.. 171

1 Close Encounters of the Oxymoronic Kinds!

As I sat on my high backed executive swivel chair going through the papers and documents placed in front of me for my signature, I was gripped by a strong emotion. If I were to pinpoint it then, I would say it wasn't a pleasant one. It was followed by a surge of restlessness. People in my position, and I was the Managing Director of a reputed company, are often revered and emulated for the kind of firmness and resilience they embody and display. Why was I then not playing my part?

Why was I engulfed with this strong feeling of restlessness? I had worked hard to reach the position I was in. The journey had not been smooth sailing, it had had its own share of challenges and difficulties and the fruit of labour should have been sweet and satisfying. Why had mine been such a short lived satisfaction? I was plagued with doubts and uncertainties. None of these stemmed from my work and inability to handle it, but ironically had a direct connection with the perfection with which I was handling it. So should not success have bred contentment? Should not perfection at work have been fulfilling? Why had discontent replaced the former and restlessness the latter?

Sitting in my plush office with the blinds open and sunlight drifting in enticingly, illuminating the interiors of my cabin and infusing it with a gentle warmth on the cold wintry morning, it was ideal for me to delve into my mind's eye.

Life they say mirrors your thoughts and ambitions and impacts the direction of your future. I travelled down the years and saw myself as a motivated, passionate youngster with a vision to conquer the corporate world. I,like most of the people did not have life's riches served on a platter and had therefore, resolved to work my way up and put in my best.

With my confidence, passion and dedication to make the best of opportunities being presented to me career wise, I would say I had done a fairly good job. This assumption of having performed well was seconded by my superiors and fructified into meaningful positions for me within the companies that I worked for. My confidence soared, my satisfaction climbed several notches higher and my bank balance developed an affinity for higher numbers. Life was smooth sailing, and I would say I had it all. But that surprisingly was not a conclusive statement and did not signal the end of my aspirations.

Twenty years of working for various companies, reporting to different bosses and then finally becoming one, was exhilarating, but the feeling was short lived. I was consumed with the desire to do something more.

I recalled my initial years of struggle when I was trying hard to establish my identity. The days I commuted by local trains in the bustling city of Mumbai, and then graduated to cabs, and then my own car. The satisfaction at that time was intense. Flash forward to today and I see myself flipping through the pages of the morning newspaper sitting on the back seat of a fancy car with a chauffeur driving me around, but the intense satisfaction has waned over the years. At the current point of time it is negligible and has been replaced by a strong feeling of discontentment and restlessness.

Being the finance guy that I was, I reasoned it out. I rarely allowed impulsive decisions and conclusions. So was it the nature of the work that was getting at me? Was it my long hours of commuting? Was it the life style of perpetually being on the go and living out of suitcases? Was it the lengthy waits at the airport lounges nibbling at tidbits and waiting for flights? Was it one of these or a combination of all as a whole?

I mulled on this for quite a while and then not having been able to come to a conclusion I decided to let this thought rest for a while. I went back to my routine tasks and then it was time for our evening review meeting. Towards the end of the meeting, just as my secretary read out the next day's agenda, I had my eureka moment. Yes I had my answer! It was the monotony of work with the same agendas, the same set of duties that I had to execute that was causing the restlessness. I had a strong feeling that it was pack up time from the company I was working for and it was time to succumb to the lure of the unknown. It was time to embark on the adventure of working on my own. It was time to use my expertise and talent in a venture that I could call my own.

I wanted to experiment once again, I wanted to take off from the launch pad of my existing career on a higher flight of success. I wanted to experience the same thrill and exhilaration that I had experienced 20 years back at the start of my career.

The seasoned professional in me tried to reason it out with the other boisterous, risk taking self and weigh the odds of this decision. The outcome I would say was not exactly encouraging.

The most challenging part of such a decision as it struck me, is the act of letting go. You have to let go of your material comforts. Your position and the perks that it brings for you. The name and fame that you acquire which is heavily weighted towards the chair that you occupy, and has less to do with your talent and innate qualities.

It took me several days to imagine a situation subsequent to me having let go and I must admit that I failed the test on many occasions. The "F" written in bold, as I donned my suit and held my office folder, ready to go back to my work and daily routine. This failure though was transient and did not last. With each passing day my earlier resolve of creating a new company that was built on my passion and enthusiasm gained ground. I started inching towards this decision and made good progress.

It was time to plan my next course of action. I had to think of the start-up. I had to make a project report with action points and most importantly plan the funding. Then came the highly trying task of breaking this news to family and some close friends. I traversed a whole gamut of emotions from people. It ranged from incredulity, to discouragement to disbelief and even laughter at this insane ridiculous thought. The reaction of incredulity and disbelief was based on the fact that an individual after acquiring all that he hankers for to lead a comfortable life, and provide the same for his family can never let go.

The nay sayers with their discouragement, spoke of only the failures and bleak prospects that I was heading towards. There were only very few people, and I could count about four on my fingertips, who said that it was an idea worth exploring and an action worth taking.

I learnt that success does not have a universal reaction. The comfort that it brings, spoils people greatly like most of my family members who were an integral part of my reflected success and they could not therefore, imagine life without it.On the other hand, there are others like me who get bitten by the exploratory bug and are raring to shake off the web of comfort that success weaves around us.

Life is a series of paradoxes and our existence interspersed with oxymorons. When you come across one, it heralds the time for you to sit back, analyze and imbibe it into your daily existence just as I did. I chose restlessness from the main course, and stopped dining on contentment that was served on a platter. I was cautioned against failure, yet decided to give up my present successes.

Was I the prodigal son, on my way to becoming a "successful failure?"

2 Turbulence–Ideas and the Situational Conflict!

As I sat on my high-backed swivel office chair that had become an indispensable part of my work life, I looked out of the window and watched the evening scene unfold in front of my eyes on the picturesque Marine drive. The wide canvas in front of my eyes was dotted with visuals. I could see couples taking a stroll, people walking their dogs, the popular "bhel and bata wada" sellers vying for the attention of the evening snack cravers. Children were seen bonding or squabbling with their friends, the office goers walking at a brisk pace, eager to return to their abodes and many other familiar scenes. There was no novclty in what I was watching; to my tired mind it was just a replay of scenes over and over again. It seemed as if all of us had become players in the wide cinemascope of life and went about our activities in a robotic manner.

My eyes wandered to the distant Arabian Sea, with its choppy muddy waters, an unsightly transformation from its original natural blue colour. I felt a strange sense of affinity and bonding with the turbulent sea. with its' warning of high tide issued and clearly visible. The ebb and flow of the waves replicated the emotions in my mind. I was at my turbulent best. As I absorbed my surroundings once again, I took note of the various certificates, awards, testimonials that adorned my office shelf and bore testimony to my performance. My cabin was replete with memories of my successes, my highs, my lows and every memory concretized to define who I was today. The successful well known Managing Director of a profitable company. Why would anybody in their sane mind choose to step down from the highest rung of the ladder to start the climb all over again?

The deep compelling feeling inside me reared its head once again and the familiar feeling of restlessness gripped me. I did not want to end up playing the same role as the characters outside my window, I determined. All of a sudden, the chair that had given me so much comfort and ease, started feeling uncomfortable and full of thorns. I knew that I had to break the shackles of my comfort zone if I were to venture into something new.

The human mind is a fertile bed of rapid emotions and thoughts as I discovered that day. When one is faced with crises and crucial decisions, a number of personalities too come out. The reasoning, practical side of me which I attribute to my financial background and expertise held me back. It was clear to me that my financial resources although comfortable at that point of time would face the risk of depletion if I broke away from a regular high paying assignment like mine. The dreamer and risk taker in me emerged and goaded me on, prompting me ahead on a path that seemed perilous yet exciting at that time.

I remember the quizzical look on the face of Shyam my office boy who was probably trying to figure out the reason for my staying back in the office. I am quite positive that he could not help but notice the computer that was switched off, the silent phone that had no call that I was attending to and the entire office staff that had left. Being a part of the characters that performed their regular duties and had no desire to question its monotony, he too accepted his part unquestioningly. When he was explained his duties, I am sure locking up the office and staying back till all the staff members had left had been explained as a part of his job responsibility.

I could hear him stifle a yawn as he came in to ask me if I wanted another cup of tea which I politely declined. I saw that intrusion too, as invasive and something that would disturb my speculation and introspection. I was lost deep in thought, combating my internal strife and seeking an answer to a question that was looming large in front of me. A question that challenged my very existence at that point - of where I was and what I wanted to be.

Gradually, with each passing minute my resolve to break away from the monotony that I was engulfed with became stronger. I was propelled towards the desire of adding a fresh, new chapter to the book of my life.

As I rolled down the blinds of my office window a task which would normally be left for the office boy Shyam, it was almost as if I was unconsciously affirming by this action of mine that it was curtains down here! Yes, my decision had been made.

There was a new found confidence in me as I bent down to pick up my files, yet another task normally done by the office boy.

It is often said that the state of your mind is mirrored in your actions, and my firm clasp on the files was indicative of that. I knew that I would be left to fend for myself without the frills of the office luxury that I currently had. Initially in any new venture I would be my own office boy and my own boss. I knew I had to take charge and break free from the addictive success and luxury of my high-profile corporate career.

My walk to the car was brisk and purposeful. My mind plagued with thoughts and the ebb and flow of emotions. Driving past the Arabian Sea, I saw the wind lashing at the waves that receded temporarily, but did not disappear completely. In fact, they came back bigger, higher and with a greater resolve to hit the shore. My resolve too had its ebb or fall and then rose again to conquer the heights of uncertainties and emerge with a stronger resolve to reach its destination.

The task in front of me was a mammoth one – winding up a corporate role and life that you have been living for many years is certainly not an easy one. I planned how I would break the news to my staff, how I would put in my papers as per the company policy and my assignment. I was thinking of how I would delegate the urgent and pending tasks. In fact, all that was needed for a smooth exit to prevent me from breaking away irresponsibly. My senior position had inculcated a great sense of responsibility which I was willing to execute to the fullest.

The next daunting task on hand was to break the news to my immediate family, my wife and young daughter.

Women they say have a strong sense of perception and a "sixth sense." My wife, I realized had sensed that despite the casual front I was trying to portray on my return home there was something which was making me uneasy. I did not want to break the news then; I had thought of creating a good preamble before doing so.

Post dinner when all three of us sat in the family room to watch TV, one hour later, I was still struggling to find a suitable opening for my speech. My wife suddenly turned around and looked me straight in the eye quizzically with a "Yes? You can tell me now." I have often wondered how somebody could be so astute and so perceptive, was it a common trait for all women or was this restricted only to a few special ones like her?

Having been left with no option but to speak my heart out at that moment, I voiced my future plans and waited for her response. A deafening silence greeted me and her expression of incredulity and disbelief made me voice the reason for my decision very categorically. I spoke of the monotony that had set in, my desire to do something different, my conviction that my passion to execute my ideas would eventually translate into success. A shrill shriek of joy greeted my ears from unexpected quarters - my daughter who had been listening to all this sprang up from the sofa and clung on to me. "Daddy, this means that you will be spending a lot of time with me. We can go on picnics, outings, just sit around and read together, get our play station out and do all the things that I have been longing to do with my darling daddy." Her firm and warm hug lifted me up. It was a symbolic act. It pulled me out of the labyrinth of my thoughts.

I turned around to face my wife, with bated breath wondering about her reaction which was yet to come.

I could see that she was lost deep in thought, probably weighing the pros and cons in her mind. The adult response is often prone to more reasoning and evaluation than that of youngsters, like my daughter's emotional and impulsive one.

Another long minute of silence and then a warm radiant smile. Yes, the brilliance of her understanding warmed my heart.

"GR I believe that you will make it, in whatever you choose to do, and I am with you." A sentence, with mere words but they signified a world of meaning. A sentence that was encouragement personified. My wife, my partner, my soul mate had given me tremendous strength and power to spur me on my new found path and decision. I was truly overwhelmed by the love and encouragement that I got from the two most important and dear members of my family.

Turbulence is crucial for change. It is the disruption and storm that propels you towards the shore; it necessitates action. A storm passes away yielding a state of calm, that is congenial for progress!

ଓ଼ଈ

3 Liberty Laced With Responsibility!

The silence of the early morning was disrupted by the sound of the alarm. The mechanical system was well suited to signal the start of the robotic chores that one performed after that. I for one, had always outsmarted the alarm, since by default I would always wake-up a few minutes before it rang. I could not however in all these years evade the robotic chores that followed after waking up. That day too,I woke up and was about to get out of bed, when realization dawned on me that I had no office to go-to. It was the first day after my resignation.

My wife's face mirrored my bewilderment. She would normally get up and cook breakfast for me and prepare my packed lunch which I would relish. As a corporate leader I had access to the VIP office canteen to eat there or enjoy the luxury of having a special canteen cooked lunch served to me in my private room, yet I chose home cooked food. Not only was it tasty but healthy too. My wife Priya, did not know what to do that morning and frankly speaking neither did I. It took me just a couple of minutes to mentally plan out my days' activities.

I could feel a strong pull from within, as if something was beckoning me towards it and that was the wonder emotion that I got up with. Just like a parent who understands the unspoken words of a new-born child, I too understood what my mind was telling me. The seeds of my new chapter in life were sown. It was time for me to water the sapling with my passion and watch it grow.

My wife Priya, was a woman of very few words. (This oxymoron was a reality and one that I could vouch for after 31 years of marriage.) Yes, she exemplified the saying "speak when you are spoken to." Seeing my resolve to get up and carry about my tasks despite not having to go-to office, prompted her to go about her duties unquestioningly. Delicious breakfast served, morning chores done, I peeped into my daughter's room, a sight which for her would the proverbial "once in a blue moon." When I told her we would all have breakfast together after which we would drive to her school to drop her off, she was delirious with joy. It takes very little to please children, I realized that day.

Their unconditional love multiplies million times over, when you give them your time and attention.

Sitting in the back seat of my car along with her, while my driver drove us to her school; her nonstop chatter was soothing and music to my ears. I realized how my time with her earlier, had to be drastically chopped off to accommodate my corporate duties. During that short drive to her school, it was as if she had unfolded and presented her whole world to me. Life for her was so uncomplicated. It moved from one friend to another, school plays, favourite teacher, sports, movies and story books. The simplicity of her world accentuated the complexity of mine. I stood at a juncture when having achieved everything in my career and having experienced its' highs I was once again standing as a newbie, waiting to explore a brand new world. I was armed only with passion and conviction that I would scale the heights of what I had in mind. My world was full of freedom, the freedom to explore as a responsible individual.

After dropping her off, I instructed my driver Das, my loyal Man Friday, to take me to a few business contacts. The idea had germinated in my mind and just needed a strong anchor then.

I had planned my day fruitfully and enthused by the surfeit of thoughts I had in mind, I went from one office to another, to introduce my ideas.

As I walked into the office of the company where I had my first meeting of the day, I saw the smiling receptionists' face lose her smile when I told her I had no business card. A confused look followed this declaration of mine, and I was pretty sure that this must have been a challenging moment for her in her job and she would recount it as one in the later years. The visiting card box kept right in front of her displayed the number of people who had come in that day. She would not receive anything from me that would add to the different shapes, sizes and logos that created an individual's paper identity in the world. She was a smart woman who quickly improvised and hastily scribbled my name and pushed it inside the box. The piece of paper was in stark contrast with the cards inside.It looked out of place, was easily identifiable and not too pleasing to the eye.

My lips curved at the corners as I smiled to myself, at a poignant thought that struck me.My smile, raised a few eyebrows, including those of the receptionist. They were all a part of the corporate world where identities were created on paper. They could not place a finger on the reason for my mirth in the absence of a proper business card for an appointment. I knew the reason for my amusement, though. The absence of a business card gave me a sense of freedom and liberty. For once

I did not want my previous identity. This meeting was the preamble for creating a brand new identity for myself.

All meetings over, it was time to take stock of the day, after I sat in my car. I mentally sifted through the results. My name was familiar and hence even without the backing of a company name, all my appointments that day materialised. After the initial exchange of pleasantries, some of my contacts were receptive, some uninterested and some rejected it half way even without giving me the opportunity to explain it fully!

Mr Malhotra, the first contact I met, heard me out very patiently and even gave his inputs intermittently during the entire conversation. I left him with the promise of him considering it and getting back to me. In short, he liked the idea and felt it was doable. Mr Sharma, whom I met next, although not downright rude, made it very clear through his barrage of questions that he was more interested in finding out why I had left my happening job and was least interested in what I would do next. Debashish's office was my next stop and he was so obsessed with his calendar and computer in front of him that he could hardly direct his gaze towards me and I knew that in his current preoccupied and disinterested state of mind, our conversation would be a nonstarter. So moving out as quickly as I had gone in, I got into my car and stopped at my last destination for the day. That meeting with Ghosh stood a fifty fifty chance of materialising I thought. He mentioned that he was very happy with my idea but did not have the time to support me then. He would no doubt look at it in the future. This to me, symbolized temporarily closing the door on my face. It wasn't closed with a thud, but closed gently and politely.

Life they say is to move on and that day symbolized it for me to the "T."

I discovered that day, that if you move with a plan, all things fall into place, I had my meeting well-planned and that day passed off very well. Those who saw me that day could see a man moving about his tasks with a determination and passion. My body language was a huge giveaway that day. My erect and attentive posture displayed my determination. My alert mind was in charge and in command. There was a heightened sense of responsibility that goaded me on to perform all my tasks that day with a new found resolve. The resolution to make my ideas succeed. The determination to pluck them out from my fertile mind and plant them in receptive grounds for them to germinate and fructify in all their glory.

My oxymoronic existence came into play sharply that day once again as I entered the house. I had stripped myself willingly off the corporate power that I had amassed over the years, yet I felt the most powerful then.

This power emanated from the power of my thoughts. That evening I felt free, I felt liberated from the monotony of clinging on to a job that did not infuse me with excitement and zeal to take it forward. While stepping into my house I was filled with enthusiasm and felt invigorated. I already had the appointments and action plan for next day chalked out!

All, ideas, including the most unique and innovative ones need the fertile soil of action and planning. The absence of these will make them inconclusive, paving the way for them to wither and die in no time!

4

Setting Sail-Donning Multihued Caps-Deck Hand to Captain!

I am of the firm conviction that the start of a journey does not herald the commitment to its' destination. For me, the most invigorating part is the germination of an idea and the subsequent planning to earmark the idea as yours, culminating in destination success.

When I set out on my start-up journey, I was raring to go like most individuals would be, when they resolve to start afresh with the thought of adding a new chapter to their respective careers.

The human mind is a powerhouse of thoughts and ideas that symbolize the very essence and purpose of one's existence. It is this powerhouse that generates the fuel for an individual's passion and success.

Armed with my thoughts and passion, I set sail on my start-up journey. I also did what I thought was very important before embarking on the voyage. I mentally discarded the garb that I was wearing from my previous corporate role. I was open to playing any role, any part that would see my venture through.

I probably went a tad bit overboard by planning to dabble in three start-ups – a triumvirate of opportunities or risks! While I was upbeat and saw it as the former, a majority of my contacts comprising friends and associates cautioned me, clearly seeing it as the latter.

It would be appropriate to mention here that my chivalry and risk taking ability had its roots in my financial background, and I believed in hedging my risks. I was inclined towards distributing my losses if any and getting out of the "all eggs in one basket" start-up syndrome.

Several rounds of discussions, sleepless nights, and long hours later I was ready with my three ventures. I was exuberant at the idea of three new companies with their bouquet of completely diverse products and services. It was in consonance with my current mood of breaking away from monotony. Diversity and passion were my new found "highs."

Like a proud parent holding his triplets in his arms, I started my parenting role responsibly. I did not want to jump headlong into the fray, I treaded gingerly, holding my babies close to my heart.I spent adequate time ideating and planning.

My first new-born was a computer training company, the second a fitness club or in common parlance a gym, and the third a financial broking firm.

While with the last one, given my background I was in familiar territory, the other two were completely alien to me. However, there was a distinct commonality in all three. They were bound with the common thread-of my resolution and passion to succeed.

Apart from the inner resolve which stems from within, a crucial part of any start-up is the USP or the unique selling proposition. So what is new in that you may ask? "We have all learned that in our marketing haven't we?" The importance of a USP is sometimes blurred or completely lost. One gets so enthused with the idea and all consuming passion of executing our projects that despite being aware of the importance of a USP, we may just wander away from it. Any business that flourishes needs the backing of a strong USP. This is the key differentiator that sets it apart from the other "Me Too" products.

Let's dwell a bit on the gym start-up. I struck upon this concept of fitness when it was neither a fad nor as well-known and popular as it is today. Yes in November 2001, this idea concretised and was sealed and stamped as a business that would probably thrive on its novelty and projected USP's.

As an entrepreneur I was keen on imbibing a few salient features in my start-ups. One of them being, shared, participative and collaborative ventures. The number one and its accompanying loneliness never attracted me. I always had partners in my companies.

Partnerships came with their pros and cons. The obvious pros being that the risk was diluted, the investments could come from different quarters and there were bouncing boards for my thoughts and plans.

The cons for me typically were that the partners I had were already well established in other ventures earning their regular bucks from those. The new ventures for them were more like hobbies which they weren't full-time into. For me, it was different. I had given up the regular bucks and my new ventures were my only career possessions and were my lifeline. This very aspect spurred me on to making all of them work since I had nothing else to fall back upon. I was answerable to my partners for their financial investments, hence had to tread very carefully.

Flashback to November 2001 when 2500 sq. ft. gyms more like "akahadas" were the order of the day. Six packs, wash board abs, toned muscles were all unfamiliar terms then. The aesthetics of the existing fitness centers that were passing off as places to exercise was in no way close to the swanky gyms that we see currently. It was very spartan and devoid of the luxury and experience that one has today.

In hindsight I derive a special sense of satisfaction when I realize that I could be credited with a lot of revolutionary ideas and experiments during my start-up days. Ideas which at that time were new and could be labelled as original.

I did away with the established norm of these small size gyms and planned to introduce a huge, spacious 20,000 – 25,000 sq. ft. gym. The gigantic gym was probably symbolic of the difference I wanted to make in the fitness industry. Ours was the franchisee of a reputed international brand and we were located in South Mumbai, an affluent, upmarket area. The stage was set for a splendid take off.

I hit upon a pioneering idea, quite a few in fact. I started a pre construction membership drive. How do you sell a service to consumers who can't see the end product you may wonder? Well, that is the crux of the win. Lace the offerings with appealing initiatives. That's exactly what I did! Shorn of all my frills and designation, I started from the lowermost rung of the corporate ladder once again. I was an integral part of the sales team. It was a unique combo role with different shades. I was executing job responsibilities of a sales executive as well as that of a boss, and there was no denying that it came with its own unique challenges. I brainstormed with my team and came up with a brilliant suggestion. Our proposed gym was close to Priyadarshini Park, so we zeroed down on the entire Marine Drive as our potential target market. All the health conscious walkers, joggers, corporate crowd, youngsters, the not so young, in fact we made no conscious demarcation. For us, the world was our oyster.

We used to start (me included) as early as 5.30 a.m. and offer fruits to the people on Marine Drive. The fruits ranged from the common ones like apples, oranges and bananas to the more exotic ones like avocados, kiwis and others. The intent here was to generate awareness about the soon to open gym. I did not believe in hard hitting "in the face "sales, and my reasoning made my team see it my way too. The fruits that we distributed became the bait to fuel curiosity about the gym. We dressed our parts with the branding of the gym and the fruits packets had catchy slogans like "If you are fit, you are a hit! " I had taken on the herculean task of committing a number of 600 memberships which in those days was a daunting task. There was nothing the members could see since the property was not constructed as yet. This successful revolutionary membership drive created another first in its duration and period of membership. Overseas, gym memberships were sold on a monthly basis while here we attempted to sell it on an annual basis. I must admit that the fitness concept then was new and unfamiliar, and the price by Indian standards - high. I was plagued with the question of whether I had adopted the right approach to sales and of course the fear of failure was looming large. We drew blanks with no enrolments initially, and then the tide turned in our favour. We started getting enquiries which translated into the much awaited enrolments. My joy knew no bounds when in precisely 3 months the numbers crossed 1000. This was much higher than my projection and expectation. With a highly motivated team we geared up for our launch!

In a lighter vein while celebrating our initial success I wondered if it had something to do with the proverbial apple and its lure for mankind albeit not restricted to the Eves in our case!

As the founder of a start-up, one gets pulled in a zillion directions. You play the Executive, the Finance manager, the HR manager and of course the Managing Director among a host of other roles.

A crystal clear vision and sharp focus in the initial days will set you on a growth path. Your vision must include a well- planned concept / ideation cycle and time frame. This is a vital factor that is crucial to success and which most Indian entrepreneur's miss out on!

Jumping headlong into the ocean of entrepreneurship will make you flounder; increase the risk of drowning and losing sight of the shore!

5 The Start-up Coexistence – Success and Debacle!

Spurred on by the early success in my fitness start-up, my fertile mind was a breeding ground for new ideas. I decided to accentuate the fitness quotient by supplementing it with more products in the same category. I thus hit upon the idea of marketing natural juices. The red, green, orange, fruits beckoned me to offer healthy natural juices to the fitness conscious frequenting the gym.

I have always maintained that for start-ups, the USP or the unique selling proposition is crucial for success. Your product or service has to stand apart from the clutter and be distinct. But fruit juices? What was so unique about that you may ask? The uniqueness here was not in the product but its' placement and the location of sale.

A gym in those days was just starting to gain popularity and hence this concept of the availability of fresh juices was a novelty and very unique then. The first day we did extremely well, in terms of sales we made a handsome 10,000 Rs. I was very satisfied with this new introduction and gave a pat on the back to myself for introducing a product without the labour of marketing and promotion to a readymade fitness conscious customer base. My joy though was short lived. The next couple of days, the sales dwindled from 10,000 Rs a day to as low as 400 and 200 Rs. Far from being profitable or a no profit no loss kind of business; we ended up making huge losses.

The initial euphoria ebbed away, exposing the ugly sight of failure. My mind was plagued with questions on what had gone wrong with what I thought was a brilliant idea. Several rounds of discussion and brainstorming with my team, coupled with my own analysis and reasoning revealed one of the biggest misjudgements that I had probably made.

The product or service as I discovered should be in keeping with the customers' expectations. Most of the clients coming to the gym had their roots in the Indian culture, where tea or "chai" was served early in the morning. Juices for Indians was certainly not a part of the early morning breakfast regimen. The customers flocked to the huge water dispensers that we had at the gym and preferred the complimentary water over the paid juices as their beverage once inside the gym.

The novelty and curiosity to try out the new introduction was probably the reason for the high sales in the initial days. It then gave way to the mindset of seeing juices as non-essential food items. There were several customers; I recall, who suddenly donned the mantle of health experts advising their fellow members to drink large amounts of water to cleanse their system after work outs. They encouraged them to assemble outside near the tea stalls, for "chai pey charcha" extolling the age old tradition of creating the strong foundation for friendship, bonhomie and good health over tea. It is interesting to note how the herd mentality in people becomes very pronounced now and then. This was one such occasion where a few led and the others unquestioningly followed. The lure of the colourful fruits waned in comparison to the watery tea.

This failure reinstated something which I already knew. The importance of research, before introducing any product. A study of the customer's behavior and preference patterns is an absolute must.

Your ideas may be brilliant and appealing but the customer is eventually the king and they decide on its efficacy which ultimately either makes it a success or failure.

If success has different dimensions, so does failure. I was to discover this much to my chagrin, after the introduction of my other seemingly bright idea. I introduced martial arts training for women, with the idea of gearing them adequately towards self-defense. I gave myself full marks for coming up with a very unique idea something that had hitherto been unheard of and I pictured this as a huge success with women taking to it as fish to water. I flew in the best instructor from the US and topped this offer with the mouth-watering words -“complimentary sessions for women.” An irresistible offer, a fantastic USP, a readymade customer base, no added marketing costs – in fact the stage was all set! This time too I was greeted by the dark side of failure. The idea did not appeal to women and found no takers. The instructor from the US was aghast at the poor response and wondered why even the “free” word could not work its magic.

Back to the drawing board and a few brainstorming sessions later, we had our answer. This concept at that time was too new. Women were comfortable with yoga and other routine exercises, but this had thrown the big question mark at them wondering if they could do it. Self-doubts, novelty, inopportune timing or a combination of all these, call it what you may, all snowballed into failure.

Success teaches you numerous lessons and so does failure. The uniqueness of failure is that it makes you hunger for success. My natural juices failure egged me on in my subconscious mind to make the concept work. This idea with the passage of time was ready to be delivered once again. I reintroduced the natural juices under a different brand name and at a unique location – a shopping mall! The juices were placed strategically at a point that was meant for family gatherings, impulse buying and social dos. The juices were the healthy options that scored over their fizzy counterparts. This venture was a clear winner and I made huge profits. The product was the same but the placement and change in the marketing strategy made that essential world of difference.

Moving on to my other venture of the computer training company, the quest for the elusive USP assumed large proportions. There were already big and established names in India and I was wondering how we would fare in comparison, The products in terms of courses were the same. The certification courses were conducted by Microsoft, Intel, and IBM. The certificate courses in hardware and software included CISCO, Oracle, Red Hat, Ethical hacking, cyber security. Even the best thinking minds could not possibly draw differentiators here, since the courses running at all institutes were identical. The key once again for me, lay in the marketing strategy and placement.

I decided to skip the Indian overcrowded software training market with its established players and establish training facilities outside India. I decided to set it up in countries where the demand for these would be higher because of non-availability so far. It was a tricky decision which ran the very high risk of uncertainty, but I chose to meet that headlong. I took the decision of setting up franchisees in faraway Nigeria, Rwanda, Ghana, Ethiopia, South Africa, Congo, Sudan, Zimbabwe. I then further expanded to The Gulf – Bahrain, UAE, Qatar and Saudi Arabia.

We ventured on untrodden land and emerged market leaders with deep global footprints of 30 successful franchisees overseas. This risk taking initiative planted the rewards of leadership and profitability in our oversize caps.

My third baby—the broking business, was again placed in an overcrowded market. The growing possibility of an existential crisis with wafer thin margins stared me in the eye. Time was ripe once again for me to change my strategy. Wc cmbarked on Debt Market Intermediation and Debt derivatives intermediation. This field had very few players. The reason could be attributed to the esoteric products being offered with the balance tipped towards the institution based placements and a B2B model. This was unlike the B2C model with equity broking with very low or nil margins. I still experience a surge of elation, as I recall how we created the No.1 debt broking firm in the country. The USP here being the unique debt product offerings to foreign banks, public sector banks and financial institutions.

It is time to face the hard and bleak truth that start-ups do fail. The ratio of success and failure varies from one entrepreneur to another. For some, it may be 9 successes and 1 failure for others it may be the exact opposite with 1 success and 9 failures, while there may be a few who tread the middle path with an equal ratio of success and failures. There is no benchmark or proven statistics for the number of start-up successes and failures that an entrepreneur might have. The right market coupled with the right customers very often, proves to be the clincher!

Both successes and failures come with their own unique learnings. While successes spur you on to greater successes, failures by giving you the must needed harsh dose of reality now and then, spur you on to replace them with successes!

A hard hitting fact of start-up success is the mantra of the right market and effective marketing strategy. The product may be perfect, but choosing a suitable market and a receptive customer base is what the entrepreneurial eye must glean!

6

Fitting the People Pieces in the Start-up Jigsaw Puzzle

The modern-day changing dynamics of the business world with a strong focus on automation and dismissal of manual tasks and interventions make me sit back and reflect. In my scheme of things, the people pieces join to provide the crucial centerpiece. They bring about coherence with their vital locks and interlocks that conjoin the other scattered pieces to complete the picture.

I go with the adage of "people make or break organizations." As start-up founders, most of us are subjected to the magnetic pull of the word "best." We want to give it our best shot, we conjure the best outcomes of our efforts in our minds, we want the best brand presence and even want to hire the best people. There is probably nothing amiss at face value with this fixation with the word best as most of us would argue. Delve deeper into it as I did, and then you realize its repercussions. These manifest themselves as soon as you are past the start line in the best people game.

In the computer training institute start-up, the lure of paper qualifications from premier colleges/ universities were the job clinchers. I remember the interview day when Amar walked in. He had an air of confidence, and his hand held the source of his confidence – his degrees and certificates from the top college of the country. As for me, my well-prepared questions could not be voiced as they were silenced by the brightness of the papers placed in front of me. A few minutes later, the meeting concluded in a rather unprecedented manner. Amar donned the cap of the interviewer and I was the interviewee where I had to answer uncomfortable questions on what offer I could make to suit his invisible premier college halo, illuminating his presence in the room. I had to even come up with a convincing answer on what career prospects I envisioned for him in the company five years down the line. I must have fared pretty well in the interview since he agreed to join us. I

followed up his recruitment with other similar ones till all my employee positions were filled up and we were ready to go ahead full throttle.

The heady excitement that I felt waned by the time it reached my senior employees and completely dwindled and almost became non-existent by the time it reached the juniors. Realization set in that the senior and "well labelled" people I had employed had jagged edges to their pieces and could not interlock with the other people pieces. Bluntly put, they were complete misfits. Their educational background came with the additional qualification of self-glorification which they exercised to the fullest. They made comparisons galore, setting off the unhealthy spiral of self-doubt and demotivation in the other employees. Month ends and review meetings would reveal unmet targets, a shortfall in the projected sales, blame games, frayed tempers and losses in revenue. This was certainly something which a start-up could not ignore and least of all me as the start-up founder. My partners for whom this was not a full-time venture had the time and inclination to pay attention to only the revenue section. As for me it was my full-time occupation and main focus and losses and non-profitability were definitely unpardonable. It did not take too long for me to figure out that I had gone completely wrong in the hiring activity. My senior employees were well labelled but not well fueled. They lacked the passion and dedication that was needed for a start-up and the proverbial "fire in the belly." It was a question of expectations from either side which remained grossly unfulfilled. The heavy timely pay packets and wielding of authority they had in mind clashed with our start-up teething troubles of erratic salary disbursals, that were heavily dependent on sales.The lack of team player spirit that they displayed and we had no room for, stemmed from their degree acquired halos.

It is one thing to realize the problem and another to do away with it on the double.

Thankfully, I fared well on this account and changed tracks as soon as this realization engulfed me.

This venture had failed, and I was not letting that set a precedent for my other ventures. The conviction to succeed and the strong desire to make a new beginning, was all I had when I started afresh after a while. This time, the hiring process was infused with a different perspective. The paper qualifications assumed a lesser significance. As the interviewer, I was calling the shots and not offering a rosy glossy painted picture of the start-up that I was heading.

I looked Swara in the eye when I told her that we would probably not be able to pay salaries on time. We would probably not be adhering to the 9 am clock in and 5 pm clock out time on most occasions, since the job at hand and its completion would overshadow the time of office closure. I repeated this to Anil and the other candidates whom I hired. I set the expectations right this time, without the tinted glasses of unrealistic expectations.

I felt confident and very much at ease when I did not have to play-act. The days progressed and we were met with routine challenges, some expected, some totally unexpected. I remember the days when I juggled the various hats of a mentor, a friend, a guide, a confidante, for my employees. There was no demarcation line between "yours" and "mine" the struggle, the losses the wins were all "ours." Swara and Anil amongst the many others never questioned the delay in payments, the no holiday work culture, the extended office hours, because their crystal clear vision could see the company in all its threadbare reality shorn off any accessories. Their motivation was a combination of extrinsic and intrinsic forces. A strong desire to perform well and put in concentrated and focused hours of work to achieve outcomes emerged. A healthy bonding, camaraderie and team spirit to tide over crises and celebrate achievements and successes together was clearly visible. The various hues of this congenial employee spirit got embedded in the colourful mosaic of the new work culture.

Is the make or break spirit of a start-up influenced only by its employees? I would say a vehement NO. The founders and leaders have an equally important role to play. The word start-up should reflect in the role and attitude of the founders and the leaders as well. You need to start your corporate journey as an entrepreneur once again. The past baggage needs to be offloaded and a fresh beginning needs to be made. The right attitude needs to be inculcated, which leaves no room for glorified designations and high handedness. The founders and partners must lead by example and display a healthy team spirit and bonding. This will then permeate horizontally and vertically within the organization.

The start-up journey must accommodate all the people in the same boat which has set sail for the same destination. If you sense weary travellers, restless travellers or those discouraging others from travelling to the common destination, they must be dropped off and replaced with new, enthusiastic ones who will gladly mingle with the other travellers and head willingly towards the common destination. Ways of motivating employees need to be looked at closely. Stock options and performance incentives go a long way in drawing them close to your organization, ingraining a sense of belonging. An air of transparency at work further aids the spirit of participation where employees feel they are important stakeholders. The atmosphere at work should be congenial and the pressure of performance should not instil fear in employees. The founders must take special care to ensure that employees are constantly encouraged to push the envelope and figure out newer and more efficient ways of performing tasks. Life in a start-up like anywhere else should have a realistic practical approach. There will be failures and losses. One must prepare for eventualities and try and minimize them through brainstorming and good crisis management. Transparency works wonders in resolving issues and care must be taken to ensure that miscommunication or lack of it does not allow negativity to seep in amongst the employees.

The focus of most entrepreneur's unfortunately is on products, and quick revenue. They lose sight of the people in the process. While hiring employees, it may be hard to fight the lure of their attractive paper qualifications. It may be difficult to be honest with them about the pitfalls of a start-up including the cash flows.

As a start-up founder, separating the wheat from the chaff assumes great significance. Paper qualifications by themselves are not the key to success while hiring employees. Qualifications, combined with passion and the right attitude will create winners in the organization.

An organization is a living entity that grows with healthy people who harbour the right attitude! Finding the right fit for employees makes the organization a perfect fit for success!

7

Sowing Ideas for Success in the Fertile Start-up Ground, Paying Heed to the Seasons

A very unique thing about entrepreneurship, especially Indian entrepreneurship is the haste for the immediate encashment of each eureka moment. As entrepreneur's, we give undue importance to the idea or the seed alone with scant regard for the season or time of its plantation. Entrepreneurship in my opinion imitates nature. All seeds have the potential of fruition that is influenced by the right season otherwise they meet an untimely demise.

As I travel down memory lane, I dwell on my fitness start-up. In 2002, when the concept of fitness as a business had not made forays into the Indian business scenario, I was enthused with building it as a concept and taking it from the existing "akhadas" stage to a sophisticated lucrative business proposition stage with a successful conclusion.

The seed of gentrifying exercise and planting it in the fertile ground of the middle, upper middle and elite class lifestyle was ready. The nascent, unstructured beginnings of the fitness industry then and envisioning it as a comprehensive ecosystem in the future was the driving force for me. The fitness start-up was well-planned and followed a natural progression from the ideation to conclusion.

The master franchisee that I opted for was an international and reputed brand in fitness. It stood on the firm ground of my deep research and exhaustive deliberations. The 2500 sq. feet cubby holes that were passing off as gyms then, had to compete with 25,000 sq. feet of space, world class equipment, qualified trainers, well defined processes and techniques. The icing on the cake was the beautiful view it had as well as the appealing, well done up interiors.

The stage was set for success and it never eluded us. I had infused the project with my heart and soul. My passion and dedication I guess outbeat the possibilities of failure. Unlike my partners who had invested in it as a hobby, for me it was my

life line. With nothing to fall back upon as a source of livelihood at that stage there was no room for failure. I firmly believe that efforts channelised in the right direction with proper planning always succeed. The gym had the perfect launch pad and started doing exceedingly well.

Success is heady and contagious. It motivates you to dream bigger, dream higher and keep stacking up your pile of success stories. I was no different. The next seeds that germinated in my bed of ideas was the desire to introduce fresh and natural juices to my existing customer base at the gym and to introduce martial arts and self-defense techniques for women at the gym. The trainer was flown in from the USA but this plan found no takers. The women were all pro yoga and meditation and something as radical as self-defense and martial arts wasn't well received or appealing at all for them. The trainer from the USA also despaired at seeing how the women made no effort to even try it out. This was a classic case of something that had started with a bang and had ended with a whimper.

The other idea, of natural juices I felt was a smart idea indeed, no investment, no marketing, just placing the product in the gyms for the consumers. The first day of introduction and curiosity raged high with beelines to the juice counter and very high sales. My team was greatly motivated, but the pat on my back had not even come in when the next day registered a steep decline in sales. Attributing it to the uncertainties of business we refused to let our spirits get dampened. The passing of time however forced us to come to terms with the fact that we were incurring heavy losses and the idea was just not working. The psyche of the Indian and gym customers was not researched and studied. It was the eureka moment which I in my haste had jumped into. The Indian mindset recognizes tea and coffee as a morning beverage and not juices. The morning tea or "chai" is so deeply ingrained in the Indian mindset that there is no room for juices to come in. The customers preferred the complimentary water at the gyms to the paid juices. We had to wind up that business incurring heavy losses as it was no longer "juicy."

After a few years in 2012, and well recovered from these failed experiences, I was armed with the idea of re-starting the juice business. Learning from my past mistake I had planned a completely different strategy this time. A result-oriented approach based on a study of the consumer mentality and a different positioning was my game plan this time.

The same product – natural juices were now placed in malls with the highest family footfalls. The juices were positioned as a luxury and entertainment product. Its multihued appeal for children attracted family gatherings and impulse buying. The children were attracted to its packaging, the parents to its health benefits and we were attracted to the ringing sound of the cash registers.

As Ravi the manager at the mall handed over the month end sales report to me, I was engulfed with the desire to impart an impromptu tutorial to him. Ravi had been a part of my gym sales team and had witnessed the earlier juice debacle. I could sense the unspoken questions and the stray thoughts crowding his mind.

I thought it was only right to explain what was plaguing my mind as well and share it with him.

"Well, you see Ravi, our earlier idea rested on a misfounded assumption of consumer acceptance. We were very sure that the positioning of natural juices as healthy options would guarantee us good sales. We were mistaken, since consumers at that time early morning are more inclined towards tea. "Chai" as an early morning beverage is so deeply ingrained in the Indian mindset that natural juices will take a long time to erode that. The positioning and strategy were all wrong there.

The mall on the other hand sees the same consumer coming in with a different mindset. They are more pro spending, they are attracted by healthy options for their children, and this assumes the proportion of an entertainment and impulse buying decision. The product is the same but the season is not. The season at the gym was influenced by the winters of caution, the cold breeze of firm decisions not to splurge on nonessentials. The seed was sown in the wrong season and it could not germinate on the frosty surface.

The seed in the mall was sown during the summer of contentment, watered by family togetherness and bonding. The warm summer breeze of happiness saw the germination of the seed here. Being armed with ideas or seeds Ravi, does not work in isolation. The strategy to plant it in the appropriate and congenial season is of paramount importance. Don't plant an idea whose time has not yet come!" As Ravi shook hands and took my leave, I could sense the dawn of understanding and his acceptance of the new found wisdom imparted by me.

Our association with our companies and start-ups is also influenced by the change of seasons. A successful start-up follows the full cycle of spring, not summer, autumn and winter. Our initial successes herald the best that spring has to offer, then we have summer where we are fully equipped to cater to the challenges and devise ways and means of surviving the heat of work pressures. We then move on to autumn, where we adopt a different mindset to brave the challenges. Winter draws on our inner strength, planning, and the company's resilience to brave odds and survive. Oddly enough, most entrepreneur's share a strong bond with their start-ups, well nothing wrong with that you would say, but I am talking about an obsession which is unhealthy. As an entrepreneur you must have the ability to dissociate yourself completely when the time is ripe without incurring life threatening pangs. We cling on to start-ups when they have scaled up and it is our time to exit. They have to survive on their own, since our role is over and we must move on. This is a difficult step to take but must be taken for the start-up to function and sustain well. The next instance which is also wrong is when the start-up is unhealthy and cannot scale up we must understand that it is time to wind up and shut shop. There is no point in carrying a burden on our shoulders when there is no hope of recovery. The third scenario is when your start-up is a profitable venture you could consider its sale. This will be a scale to sell as against a scale to exit.

Products, planning, strategy, customers, all have their places earmarked and each has to be considered in its individual capacity and then as a holistic picture.

A product may be exceptionally good, but unless evaluated on the grounds of its acceptability by the customer and without any proper planning it is bound to fail.

Seeds and ideas are unique and need the fertile ground of the customer mindset to germinate and flourish, provided they are planted in the right season that is congenial for their fruition.

Every seed has a season and is planted for a reason!

8

Choosing People Wisely—Those Who Fan the Embers of the Start-up Fire Instead of Dousing Its' Flames!

The oft used cliché that people are the soul of start-ups is undoubtedly true as I discovered. Having forayed into my computer training start-up the next crucial step was to hire people for it. I had the grandiose vision like most start-up owners of establishing a path breaking company. If the vision was magnificent everything related to it would have to be the best too. With this as my guiding force, I set about my task of hiring employees from the top colleges with the highest marks and best track records.

After a 15-day exercise of scanning numerous resumes, spending hours on the phone talking to prospective candidates, doing reference checks, it was time for the last and final step of personal interviews.

As I sat looking at Atul (whom I was contemplating for a senior position) seated opposite me in the board room, I went through a quick mental recap of the questions I would ask him, but before I could voice the first one, I heard the sound of his voice "Sir, have you chartered out a strategy for the next two years? Growth plans? consumer mapping? Is a competitor review in place? I would be happy to see a project report of this company so that I could then implement what I have in mind for the next two years or so ...... and more and more questions came flooding in.

Hold on, wait, what about my questions? They remained unanswered as questions that could never be asked. The interview which I had planned did take place but the tables were indeed turned. I was the interviewee and Atul the interviewer.

The next 3 – 4 candidates I had selected also had questions of their own but thankfully, I could get some of mine across. The enthusiasm with which I had started the interview dwindled a little giving way to self-doubt and apprehension. I was a bit fazed at the thought of how I would cope with such intelligent and vocal employees armed with the best in paper qualifications.

The tea break gave me some reprieve as I had time to ponder and debate with myself if I was making the right decisions on the hiring aspect. Then realization dawned in my cloudy mind, that if these were the best, they would be necessarily different from the run of the mill yes sir no sir candidates, they would have a mind of their own and a different perspective towards a new job. Taking some solace in that thought, I was now ready to close the final stage – the pay package or salary. Back at the negotiating table, a calculator and notepad in hand, the final discussions were on with Atul. Like in most negotiations it was a give and take and then a common ground was discovered to the satisfaction of both parties. One question that loomed large on my mind however, was Atul's query of how as a start-up I would be able to afford the offered salary. Under any other circumstance I would have construed this as an affront but I was in a hurry to hire the best so had to let him into the confidential details about the financial backing of the company to appease his doubts. I made a herculean effort to conceal my keenness bordering on desperation to have him on board.

The customary handshake, transfer of signatures and my team was in place. I felt triumphant that I had as a start-up managed to get the best in the industry as my senior personnel.

Work started as planned, I would come to office, we would have the routine meetings, firefighting, instances when we would all emerge unscathed as a company and get back to more work the next day. I was consumed with the heady pace of a start-up, till one fine day I heard alarm bells. The unpleasant sound of these warning bells indicated losses, client drop outs, decline in revenue and business forecast that did not look promising at all.

As I sat on my swivel chair in my cabin looking out of the glass door, I could see my employees engaged in animated conversation, with despondent faces. I was curious but short of barging in and confronting them on the subject of their conversation, how could I come to know what was happening I wondered. I then thought of handling it in a dignified way befitting the CEO of the company. I called Atul inside on the pretext of some work and then asked him to have a cup of tea with me. Well into five sips of tea and it was time for my question. I asked him about the despondent looks on the faces of the employees and what the topic of the conversation was. Atul in his authoritative style assured me that all was well and he was in command. I took the only option that I had then – I believed him!

The subsequent days too, yielded the same results, work and business started going steeply downhill. What was happening I wondered, hadn't Atul told me he was handling it and there was no cause for concern? Didn't I have the best in the industry as my senior manager? A person whose paper qualifications, and track record were nothing short of the best? I decided to give it some more time and leave it in the able hands of Atul. After all faith and delegation were also essential aspects for a start-up owner and I wanted to live up to that.

After a recent sales meeting with heavy losses and a rather scanty customer base, I knew it was time for me to come down with a heavy hand. There was something wrong somewhere and I had to find the hole and plug it.

I decided to speak to the team without Atul, in a bid to explore another perspective. The opportunity presented itself very soon when Atul had to leave for a client meeting. The small board room that day housed many quizzical faces, as I addressed them and asked them what were the reasons for our losses despite the infrastructure support and everything else that was needed from the company's end being in place. Over a two-hour conversation what emerged was indeed very shocking and something that shook me up. I learnt that Atul had been delegating his tasks to his juniors and not following it through. He was gradually gnawing into their self-confidence through his doubts and uncertainties about the company's standing. Atul was constantly placing himself on a pedestal and undermining the capabilities of the others. He was even going to the extent of openly admonishing them for their incompetence which was more often than not misplaced.

Physically he would be present at work, but mentally he would be completely switched off. He would only discuss how a start-up would be doomed amongst the bigger players and how it was futile to even try and vie for business. The smallest challenge would be hyped up and made to look as the most impossible task.

Initially, after he had joined, he had given it his best shot and the progress of the company was also good, well on the path of progress, but a few months into this job and he felt he was suited for a better company and a better salary. Efforts diminished, targets were not met, revenue dwindled as a result of which salaries were delayed.

Atul started gnawing into the self-confidence of the other employees and stopped contributing towards the company's growth. He displayed an air of nonchalance; he was aware that his paper qualifications stood strongly between him and the door of dismissal. Even after knowing the truth, I did not want to rock the boat. I was like the boatman who knew that the oars were defective and I had slim chances of weathering the stormy turbulence of the sea, yet I was looking up at the sky waiting for the sun to shine through and calm the storm. I did not and could not throw away the oars. The oars were an indispensable part of the boat. I wanted the best and had got the best in terms of appearances not functionality.

Finally, by a stroke of immense good luck the sun shone through! This sunlight was different. The light that emanated was not to calm the storm, but it was the light of understanding that calmed my troubled mind. It was the light of introspection. It was the wonderful light that illuminated my mind and made my thoughts crystal clear. Yes, it was time to act!

My gait the next day at work embodied a sense of purpose, a determination which had been missing on the previous day. I summoned Atul to my cabin and confronted him with what I had heard and understood from the others. His facial expressions displayed a saga of emotions which left no doubt in my mind about the authenticity of the information received from the team.

An exchange of signatures and a last working date stamped and sealed on paper. He had completed his cycle of employment here, albeit a bit prematurely. This experience was undoubtedely marked with a home truth. It culminated in valuable lessons for both of us.

Paper qualifications do not guarantee the best selection of a candidate and mere possession of paper qualifications by a candidate do not guarantee infallibility at work!

9

Reinventing People Dynamics and Seasoning It With Experience!

The progression of an entrepreneurial journey comes with the life jacket of experience that ensures that the learning that you amass prevents you from drowning in the sea of uncertainties and challenges. The vision of most entrepreneur's is a pin hole vision focused on the product and its USP'S which they are almost certain is the defining factor of a start-up's success. In my opinion, a product although important is inanimate, and needs a vibrancy to bring it to life. While focusing on creating a halo effect for the consumer, one must also work towards establishing the company as a living entity. This pulsating entity then, has a nerve center – people or team members.

Having experienced the debacle of hiring heavy weights in my earlier start-up, I had now trained my eye and tuned my mind to look beyond the sheen of paper qualifications. I was armed with the certainty and knowledge based on my past experiences, that impressive backgrounds and high qualifications do not come with the assurance of good performance. I was determined to fine tune and add different parameters in my search for suitable candidates.

As I sat in my cabin initiating the recruitment process once again, it was ironical that the qualifications and degrees that were presented to me by the candidates, remained where they were – on paper!

In my mind's eye I was keenly observing the body language of the candidates and their tone, their enunciation, their voice modulation, their body language all the crucial indicators that guarantee the proverbial "fire in the belly" accompanied by a sparkle in the eye.

I realized that learning is an ongoing process which never plateaus. It envelopes everyone within its ambit, be it a boss or a subordinate. As a boss I had learned the art of sieving the wheat from the chaff in the hiring process by changing my pre set definitions and rearranging them to suit the start-up culture.

Jatin, Rehan, Sheetal, Ruhi, and Saransh now formed my new team. As I told the office boy to file their resumes, a sense of satisfaction enveloped me. This time, I wasn't burdened with the task of creating a larger-than-life picture of my start-up. In the earlier instance, so consumed was I by my passion to hire the best from the best colleges that I had painted a rosy and attractive picture of my start-up. I had promised and committed to salaries that were very high and ended up creating a top-heavy company. This threatened the very balance of the foundation stone crucial for any start-up. I had created the risk of it toppling over and topple over it did, resulting in a failed company because of its team.

The foundation stone laid this time was on transparency, in a boss – subordinate relationship. I had elucidated to the team of new recruits that a start-up is submerged in a sea of uncertainties. Closely intertwined in a start-up ethos are delayed salaries, long working hours, the risk of no holidays, coming to work on holidays and many more. A start-up journey in fact, mimics a roller coaster ride quite accurately.

The team heard me in silence absorbing each and every word that I said, probably they too were judging the genuineness and sincerity in my words and body language. I must have scored well there, since all of them signed the appointment letters and started work.

The air at work was rife with enthusiasm and lightheartedness. The desire to perform and outshine in their respective jobs was important to these newbies. I felt drawn towards this style of working and traded my role of the owner – and founder with that of their colleague sans any designation.

I remember the gleam in their eyes when I used to sit with them bouncing ideas, brainstorming and occasionally stretching out my arm to take a bite of the home-made sandwich that lay so temptingly in an open tiffin box of one of the team members. A sense of camaraderie blossomed which pointed towards guaranteed productivity. I was enjoying my role with multiple hats, one for each official role. I transited from an accountant to a sales person to an HR person to a marketing person. I slid into a multitude of roles to keep the process smooth and running.

Work picked up, we started getting new orders and developed many clients. I was happy that I did not have to stay put in my chair and relive the truth of “1 is a lonely number”or how lonely it was at the top. I was hands-on and enjoying it.

When things are moving very smoothly in life a disruptor is not far behind, and will ensure that the smoothness is hampered in one way or another. Ours too, came about in a most unexpected way. We were two partners in the start-up and shared a bond that had grown over 18 years. A togetherness that had stood the test of time and developed into a strong relationship. We were soon to realize how wrong we were in presuming that.

It was after a routine review meeting and after each team and individual had presented their work, that something untoward happened. My partner Ravi Mehta, who was more of an impatient investor, than an active professional involved with the day-to-day work, reprimanded the sales team for under performance. He said that they did not know how to clinch deals. The impatience of Ravi was countered by the sharpness and boldness of Rehan. Having heard the repeat sentence and words of "none of you know how to clinch a deal" "how unsmart you are"and other such unflattering talk, Rehan reacted with a childlike innocence which he to this day maintains was genuine curiosity. He asked Ravi for a practical live demonstration on cracking a deal. He requested him to demonstrate and assured him that they were quick learners, would learn and follow suit. Ravi was completely taken aback at this reply, since he was old school and always wanted seniority and experience to take precedence in communication with employees. In his world of don'ts therefore, employees never challenged or gave instructions to their bosses. They never sat together and had meals, they never went on sales calls together, in fact his world was teeming with a million don'ts. What Rehan had just suggested was unthinkable and unheard of in Ravi's owner driven employee engagement world. Subsequently, in a very high-handed tone he informed the team that he had other more important things to do, hence he would not try and clinch a deal at an employee's behest.

He told me to hand out a warning and dismissal letter to Rehan for audacity and insubordination. I tried to reason out with him to tell him that this did not seem like an engineered argument etc. but he wasn't willing to listen. 18 years were snapped in a jiffy when he hurled the accusation of partiality towards the employees at me and walked out of the company on that day both literally and figuratively. He wanted me to sack the boy immediately and my failure to do so had prompted his permanent departure, snapping a bond that we thought was a very strong one.

Quite unwittingly though, that day I coined a proverb which roughly translates to, if owners and top people lose money that's experience, but if the juniors or the professionals in the team do the same thing it is immediately attributed to their ignorance and lack of experience.

I pride myself on being an eternal optimist. I feel after every failure there is a win, every cloud has a silver lining and inexperienced people, pitted against the background of experience will emerge successful. Ordinary people can surely do extra ordinary things if we have a plan in place.

I also opine rather vehemently that the involvement of employees is very crucial in a company's process and this can be ideally done by cultivating a sense of belonging. The first few employees who have stayed through thick and thin have weathered the uncertainties of delayed salaries, losses, giving up on family togetherness and occasions only because they had to be at work, need to be rewarded with equity. Other employees who join down the line can have their usual target related bonuses and incentives to encourage a sense of participation and belonging that will herald company growth and positivity.

The company culture should be performance driven and enthuse the employees to report to work every day out of a willingness born out of their love for the company rather than the fear of salary cuts. They must enjoy working in the company and create a great place to work culture instead of just a good company and brand. People are important and people skills is an art that needs to be mastered by all alike.

Entrepreneur's must subscribe to the veracity of "the man of words and commitment once given cannot be broken" philosophy. They must only promise what they mean to their employees. No empty words, no inaction. Action is the need of the hour in start-ups, more so, I would say than other types of companies and industry.

Another essential learning that I gathered was the need of any owner to tone down their lifestyle in accordance with the financial situation of the start-up. The owners' personal expenditure on salaries, petrol, travel, business class, private jets, super luxury cars, should not give the employees a chance to accuse employers of maintaining double standards. One to show the employees and one for their friends and family. Being ethical and transparent will ensure employee loyalty.

People dynamics and mastering it will unleash a deep understanding of self, of the others around you and the organization.

Good people skills will ensure adapting and connecting with the company environment. It will influence team behavior positively. Team performance will also receive a fillip in the right direction. Good communication and transparency will go a long way in ensuring a good company culture!

A start-up has many doors that open up one by one and lead to the throne of success. The first door opens with a key that is cast in the mould of an engaged, involved and motivated team of employees!

10 The Go-to-market Strategy—the Nerve Center of All Start-ups!

I have always bracketed myself in the anti-cliché squad, but this is one instance when I make a deviation. A deviation backed by years of experience and knowledge, as I vouch for the GTM.

While being passionate about your product, having that unique idea which propels you to take the bull by the horns and jump into the fighting arena is an excellent starting point. The ground work or preparedness for it, precedes the entire take off process.

A go-to-market strategy signifies a clarity of vision and purpose which goes a long way in preventing the untimely demise of a start-up and helps take it to its full potential.

A word of caution here, an effective go-to-market strategy may not guarantee success but at least it will ensure that the product gets all the lifelines it needs to stay afloat in the turbulent sea of expectations. A combination of several other factors then come into play, which decide whether it crosses the dark deep ocean to reach the shore successfully or not.

Tracing the journey of all the start-ups I was involved with; I realized that the biggest hitch was the fear of embarking into the unknown. It was like setting sail but not knowing the temperament of the sea and what kind of weather lay ahead.

So, then what does one do in the face of this fear? The answer quite simply lies in being equipped with the best tools and navigation aids to help you weather the storm and come out unscathed.

Surveying the market, testing your products and understanding the customers are the pre requisites that any start-up must treat with reverence. One cannot jump into the fray armed only with good ideas and good products.

A GTM (Go-To-Market) strategy is the precusor to a good product launch. The unveiling of a product needs to be coupled with a well-researched, fact-based plan that eliminates the risk of chasing the wrong audience, or a premature or late product introduction, targeting a saturated market. Most importantly, not wasting time, resources and man power in a fruitless chase.

These inherent risks accompany any start-up and a well-crafted plan for these potentially disastrous hitches and road blocks offer magical benefits.

To avoid these potentially disastrous glitches and hang-ups, you need to craft an actionable, thoughtful and very effective go-to-market strategy. One must also be prepared to understand that this may not be smooth sailing as the process itself, is not an easy one to navigate. At the end of it however, there is the unparalleled thrill of achievement if successful or deep learning if it does not meet with the planned success. Either which way you emerge victorious with rewards to cherish.

Let me once again take you back to my wellness start-up and recall the lesson learnt. We had hit the jackpot with a unique fitness concept – self-defense for women keyed into the fitness regime enhancing the value and benefits!

The team was riding high on the crest of a hitherto unknown concept. We went ahead full steam and spoke about it to the ladies, who were already members of our gym. The idea sadly had no takers, because independence and self-defense were unexplored territories during the early 90's when this was looked at as an alien idea. Very ironically, the novelty of the idea itself proved to be its bane. This brilliant idea took with it a colossal waste of time, investments in hiring and flying in a team of experts from overseas who would train in martial arts.

We had failed big time, by not conducting adequate research and just jumping into the fray without testing our life saving gear. We had to incur heavy losses and most sadly, the smothering of the burning flame of our enthusiasm.

Testing the market and testing the waters is very important. One must have a handy roadmap that can be used to measure the viability of an idea's success and also predict its performance on the basis of prior examples, market research and competitive data that is analyzed.

Contrary to popular belief, funding isn't the main concern and challenge. Although it is a major one. The main challenge is to find the right customers for your product or service.

As a start-up founder I realized how important it was to slip into various roles and functions with ease to set the ball rolling. There could not be distinct compartments. I had to don the cap of a sales manager accompanying my team for presentations and sales pitches, leading the way, giving my inputs and giving them a shot in the arm, motivating them to perform and close deals. I also instilled a change in their thinking process by making them understand that failure was inevitable. Not all sales pitches would go through. If failure was inevitable so was the learning from it. Needless to say, that my personal involvement and encouragement made them fare much better and dispelled many doubts and apprehensions.

I did not believe in being an armchair specialist like my partners who quite mistakenly thought that their duty was just to sit and evaluate and caution the team against failure. In my approach I was a part of every success and failure as I experienced it first hand being an integral part of the sales pitches and presentations.

I recall a very pertinent example of a GTM strategy that was on the brink of failure but bounced back with ease.

In my computer parts start-up, we went on our routine presentations and sales pitch rounds, armed with our product knowledge laced with our perfect English and vocabulary backed by our beautifully illustrated PPT for the presentation.

At the end of our presentation, we could see that we had drawn a blank and this deal looked far from positive. As we were preparing to leave, feeling dejected and low which is a natural human emotion, at the first glimpse of failure, my colleague Sathish asked to be excused. He went back in to meet the customer Mr. AK Padukone. After half an hour of waiting, we could hear loud voices followed by some laughter from Mr. Padukone's cabin. Our curiosity was awakened as we wondered what was transpiring between the potential customer for whom post our presentation, we had replaced the prefix potential with lost.

When a beaming Sathish came out he told us that he could discern what was beyond the blank look of Mr Padukone, it was not a disinterest in our products or services. It was something as simple as a roadblock of language which led to a deeper more complex blurring of comprehension and the inability to take a decision. Being a Kannadiga, when spoken to in Kannada his comprehension and understanding were at a hundred percent as against his 15 percent comprehension level of English. Convinced with the superiority of our products and based on his requirement, the deal was ours. We had to again mentally indulge in substituting prefixes, this time the lost customer became a new customer.

We had failed in conducting a GTM where a study of the customer and his public background were a prerequisite.

Another very important observation that I would like to make here is that merely having a GTM strategy doesn't conclude your marketing and sales efforts. That is not the last chapter of your sales. The most important chapter is the review and feedback for each success and failure.

Given that a go-to market strategy should have a clear, structured approach and must progress towards achieving a best fit for the company, a review is a million-dollar approach towards understanding what works and what doesn't.

It is always productive to take a few steps back after each deal, lost or won and analyze the intricacies of success and failure. Identifying a target audience, creating a marketing plan and outlining a sales strategy are the key components of a GTM strategy.

In all the start-ups that I initiated, I discovered that the GTM has certain common parameters irrespective of which industry it is charted for. The common concepts are to find the best product- market fit, find the target audience, study and research competition and also obtain a real time picture as to the demand for your product or service. It is also important to list out and plan the mediums through which the product or service will be distributed.

It is time that every start-up founder and his team understood that only a unique or superior product or service does not guarantee success. A go-to-market strategy which includes the customer, product, distribution, vis a vis competition is crucial for all start-ups.

Even the brightest of ideas need to be fanned by the winds of effective execution, so that they don't burn out, sucking the start-up into oblivion within the initial years of its existence!

11 The Start-up Misnomer–Awards vs Rewards

I have always been wary of entering an office and being escorted to a plush cabin with a wall lined up with fancy shelves bedecked with glittering trophies and awards. The employee walking me there I believe, has as part of his induction been trained to point to a chair for the visitors' seating which would give them an inescapable panoramic view of the glitter on display.

The wait for your appointment is quite obviously timed to give you that crucial glimpse of awareness and enlightenment that it would take to introduce the company's accolades and laurels to you.

As a start-up, people get hooked onto an awards strategy. According to popular belief their thinking harbours on the premise that the hiccups of finances, low customer acquisition and retention are washed down by a deluge of awards. Who does not want to be recognized and felicitated? You may ask, well almost nobody would be the answer.

Awards and recognition are deeply ingrained in a company's success story. They are also seen as providing credibility and recognition to them, but that happens after the passage of a certain time period. Awards give a big boost to company culture, morale, values, and the cohesiveness of a team.

A start-up winning numerous awards is always looked askance and most often than not, the huge array of awards defeat the purpose. The energies of the start-up team must be focused on customer acquisition and retention, deployment of resources, a go-to market strategy, product knowledge, upgradation of employee skills and other vital mandates. The widely prevalent misnomer in the start-up culture is awards instead of rewards.

If I were to make a tongue in cheek remark here, I would say without completely eliminating the rewards of the award culture, I would advocate it being tweaked to suit the start-up ethos. Rewarding employees for good work done, rewarding your customers with value added services, should be a take off point. When you sit back and look at the loyal and good customer base you have cultivated, the employee who looks forward to coming to work each day and the products and services which gain customer testimonials are your true rewards. You do not need a third-party validation at the initial phase of the start-up.

Start by building a company with pro social values, start rewarding your employees and the ideal situation of corporate and individual awards will then follow and merge meaningfully.

I remember Ajay, my Marketing Manager in my computer training start-up who swore by the concept of an awards culture to enter the radar of the customer. So consumed was he with this fool proof method of winning customers that he tried all the tricks available in the marketing hat. Numerous applications floated out, impeccable vocabulary was inculcated in the product and company write ups that were sent out to the jury members of various awards panels. Time, energy and a lot of expectation all pinned onto those glittering start-up awards. When a few calls from the award management committee came to him he was extremely excited to rattle off his rehearsed speech on how good the service of the company was and how competent the team was. The written rounds, the question and answers round, went on for many days and his enthusiasm too grew day by day. The focal point of the employee conversations during those times was on how prestigious this award would be if it came our way. His enthusiasm was contagious and rubbed off on all the other employees. As I walked around the office, I could see each calendar at the various work stations had a circle around the date of the award. I was almost certain that numerous Gods depending on the faith and religion of each employee were being invoked to shower their blessings so that after the award, we would win that elusive and rewarding clientele that would make our start-up gallop towards success. For a few employees from the marketing team this offered a short cut to actually moving out and getting customers. This award would come with the promise of eliminating the leg work and just landing a plum cake with customer toppings on to your platter. The start-up grind would then be effectively addressed to a large extent. With limited start-up resources and time this was the proverbial apple which Ajay and all other employees could not wait to take a bite off.

As I sat in my cabin taking in the sights and sounds of the employee environment, I could not help but speculate on the importance that awards and recognition had gained. It had become a symbol of attachment and a common cause to strive for. My managerial style has always been that of doling out delegation in large measures to my employees. Ajay was a senior employee and I did not let my way of thinking, my apprehensions, my doubts, cloud his perspective. His eyes were set on an award and for him the rest would be a corollary of it. I was amazed at the way he had made the others in his team too follow his line of thinking. There were no questions asked, the belief and faith was a shared and common one.

The day of the award dawned with each member of the marketing team dressed in their best suits attending the ceremony. As the Founder Director of the company, I too had a VIP pass and made it to the ceremony. Several awards later, it was time for our category to be announced. A quick look at my team, the look of anticipation and I felt a nudge at my heart strings – what if we didn't win? What if we didn't make it past the other competitors? Wouldn't it be difficult to motivate the team to work the next day? Would Ajay be plagued with doubts and uncertainties about the company? Its qualifying worth? Those 10 minutes from the time the award category was announced till the company write ups of the nominees were read out till the final announcement must have been the most trying for me. I had been detached when the entire award process was being entered into since I had my reservations about the same. Those 10 minutes however, sucked me in so deeply, that the only thing I wished for was to resurface soon and get back to a normal work routine with my team.

The look of exuberance on the faces of my team members and especially Ajay jolted me back to reality

– yes, we had done it! We had won the most promising start-up award.

The next day at work was a display of high energy, optimism and a lot of camaraderie. If the sound of high fives could shatter glass windows, we would have achieved that feat too on that day.

A couple of days later, Ajay along with a few key members from his team came up to me and announced their departure for a very important customer presentation. Their visiting cards had been redesigned to display the coveted award under the company name and logo.

I wished them well and went back to the work that I was doing. Four hours later, the team returned. Their enthusiasm, their high energy levels were low or should I say completely missing? Dismissing it as a tiring day and a long customer interaction I asked Ajay what the outcome was.

He requested that I meet him in my cabin to which I promptly agreed. Words were slow to come out as he painstakingly tried to form sentences. "We lost the deal."

These four words did throw me off balance but as a senior member of the team I had learned a few tricks of the trade, one of them being never to show your shock or surprise in front of your juniors. I measured each word before uttering it and asked him in a seemingly dispassionate way as to what had happened.

"Well Sir, they were very impressed with our presentation and service till they asked us the clincher – who are your customers? We had no answer to that. The award did mention us as a promising start-up but they were more inclined towards finalising it with the company that showed them the customer testimonials. They also made a few calls to those customers to check on the company's services."

I have always believed in and still do very vehemently that one happy customer, one good word of mouth publicity outshines the brilliance of a thousand awards.

A start-up should focus its' time and energies on rewards and not confuse it with awards!

The glitz and glamour of the awards do not necessarily illuminate the company. It is but a fleeting light that does not sustain long enough to illuminate the path of hard work that lies ahead.

The true shine of achievement comes through dedication and hard work. The desire to put in your best for your customer by adding value that is unparalleled.

The initial quest of a start-up lies in the search of that reward that illuminates its' very being and existence.

The halo of every start-up - Its valued and loyal customer base!

12 A Start-up Essential—Desperation to Conviction!

Even the most optimistic of entrepreneur's needs a harsh dose of reality now and then is what I learned, when faced with the start-up grind of my document storage company. We were aware that we were pitted against big players and giants. We had planted the sapling of our idea into an already overcrowded flower bed, yet we were convinced of its potential to flower, watered by our passion and dedication.

Real Estate in Mumbai, especially at prime locations is that elusive piece of pie which everybody wants a share of. The deeper the pocket, the more exclusive your share. The office space for our document storage company was in a prime location of Mumbai. We were aware that our operational costs were high, and our pockets were not deep. We had to move at supersonic speed towards generating decent revenue. At the month end, a sense of dismay coupled with uncertainty related to the start-ups' success plagued me. I was enveloped by the enormous monthly pay outs of a bootstrapped start-up. Holding the numerous bills in hand, little did I know that the very piece of paper with an exorbitant rental that I was looking at with dismay would be my ticket to success.

My moment of realization dawned when I reflected on the past few client meetings we had participated in to secure business. Our presentations although well structured lacked that one ingredient that would make the decision dip in our favour – a USP. We were offering what other players had already offered and were engaged in. I realized that passion and dedication were essentials but not the only ones. They needed the backing of a unique strategy or competition differentiator to initiate client interest. The rental bill that I was holding in my hand charging me for space gave me the idea of offering that very precious commodity to my clients.

I decided to give them the offer of freeing up their space, as a value proposition. Yes, this indeed would be our USP!

I decided to offer to move my clients' files to another area and free up their office space for use by their employees and for other important activities that required space. This may seem a very run of the mill, simple solution for a few of you, but those who are familiar with Mumbai and the rentals for commercials/ office space would definitely beg to differ.

After a brainstorming session with my team and a well thought out strategy, incorporating the new model, was quickly keyed into all our client presentations. As a team, we then put together our business plan, our business model and scalability.

We were desperate for business and this desperation I believe is a positive occurrence for any start-up. Desperation makes you reach within yourself and come up with novel ideas to overcome obstacles or simply to get you moving ahead in your journey. Small ideas too, can unveil big plans.

We decided to take our new plan to a large banking company. We were able to generate preliminary interest with our new found strategy. The initial hurdle crossed, we were able to graduate to senior level meetings and present our ideas there. The decision makers from the company's side were willing to try out our service, but had oodles of skepticism and doubt added to their initial approval.

Our offer was of moving all their files outside Mumbai, to Bhiwandi. While this move was an indicator of high profit margins for us by lowering our rental outflow, this very distance fueled the doubts of the clients as they wondered about the promptness of our service.

Why Bhiwandi you may ask? We had a few compelling reasons to make that particular choice. In our exercise of scouring for large spaces with cheaper rental alternatives, we realized that Mumbai offered no solutions. We would have to consider its suburbs or even beyond.

On 17 May 1984, riots had broken out in the industrial belt of Bombay, Thane, and Bhiwandi. This was a Hindu – Muslim riot and several businesses had been impacted and most had come to a grinding halt.

Our search culminated in a possible solution - a large shut down textile mill in Bhiwandi.

Desperation was our deal clincher. The owners were desperate to get some income to cope with the heavy losses that they had incurred due to the ongoing riots and closure of business. We were desperate to woo one of the largest companies to sign up with us and give us that much awaited head start.

A talk with the local union was included as a mandatory item on the agenda, and saw us accepting their terms of hiring the locals to generate employment for them. Seeing it as a bundle of opportunities, in terms of saving manpower cost, commuting cost and accommodation costs, we readily agreed. We were aware though that we would have to compromise a bit on the qualifications of the employees, as their experience and education would not be at par with those from their neighboring metro of Mumbai. Our initial doubts on this aspect were easily quashed by my partner Karan, who made a very wise statement. He mentioned that the type of work required to be done was not very high skilled. It was manual and adequate training and induction would equip the employees to carry out the tasks smoothly. After all, photocopying, numbering, filing, retrieving files that were properly stacked and labelled was no rocket science.

My mood was very upbeat as I walked into the Chairman's office to sign on the dotted line in the contract with the A list banking company. I must admit here though, that my initial exuberance suffered a huge onslaught of doubt when I was asked if we would get the documents to them in the record time of 24 hours promised by us in our service contract. I realized at that moment that desperation also ironically gives birth to conviction. Although this service was new and untried by us, I was so consumed by the passion of winning this client that I was convinced of my company's capabilities to execute this.

My conviction sadly enough did not rub off on the client. They did sign the contract but subjected it to various clauses, the foremost being our capability to conclude the trial round successfully.

It was time for our trial round. All the steps were laid out. It began with us transporting the files of the clients to our location in Bhiwandi, video recording the entire process to eliminate any doubts of its storage in Mumbai itself. We had hired SUVs for the transportation and the drop at Bhiwandi was executed effectively. The next day was our 24-hour retrieval deadline. I made my way to the client's office ready to witness our inaugural service. This was a crucial deal and my hopes and aspirations were pinned on it big time.

Fate doesn't play best buddy always, and sometimes lets you down at the most crucial junctures. This was one of those moments. Despite meticulous planning and sending out my best employees on this inaugural mission we failed in delivering the files to the clients' office in time. We missed the bus by 2 hours. There were several factors beyond our control that dampened our entire schedule and sealed our failure.

A look at the faces of the client's team members and I knew our start-up fate had met its end, at least with this company. I could not bear the thought of losing such a coveted client, a client through whom we could snowball into other sister concerns and increase our client base effortlessly with this one deal bearing testimony.

It was desperation again that made me come up with a convincing solution for the client. I proposed a 10% penalty clause on all delayed deliveries. This idea had quick takers. It made business sense to them as they believed a financial pinch would be too painful for start-ups and therefore herculean efforts would be made by us to avoid such lapses.

The joy and relief of winning that marquee client was unparalleled and it was celebration time for us. I was optimistic that we would now add to our client portfolio quite effortlessly since that one name was a heavy weight.

My next few meetings with the team were focused on tightening the loopholes, impressing upon them the consequences of delay with its financial repercussions. I was overwhelmed by the unwavering support of my team. We were in it together and worked with a new found solidarity to achieve the goal of client satisfaction.

Work progressed smoothly, my Bhiwandi team proved that knowledge of the English language contrary to popular belief was not a precursor to efficiency at work. My periodic review though, unveiled another loophole – low employee morale! There was an urgent need to plug the negativity that was hampering the positivity of the employee environment. This stemmed from the managers I had hired from Mumbai. They came with an air of superiority of big city Mumbai and could not accept the minimally qualified Bhiwandi staff, sans their knowledge of English. I decided that it was time to replace them with the local talent and salvage my business in time.

Good fortune smiled on us and my start-up became profitable and raced past the big daddies of business. As a seasoned start-up founder, I have always advocated a detached attachment. Eight years down this start-up company journey and it was time for this detachment to come into play. My profitable venture was sold to the biggest company and name before we overtook it.

I exited with a huge profit and at an opportune time. The timing of one's exit strategy is very crucial and I had made a perfect exit then. As for the fate of the penalty clause, allow me to let you into a big secret. It was never implemented! If you were thinking of complimenting us on our effectiveness and agility of execution, I will be quick to correct you. The client never once in those 8 years demanded a 24-hour turnaround time. They never needed files. In fact, their requirement was limited to a few papers which we could scan and send for reference. The audits where files were needed were planned in advance and we had ample time to transport the files. The penalty clause strategy was a reassurance for the client, it was his armor against the vagaries of our service.

The winds of desperation are inherent in a start-up journey. Successful start-ups weather these very winds bravely and remain unfazed, turning their direction, allowing them to gather momentum till they finally emerge as a tempest of their conviction!

13 Partnerships in Start-ups–Enriching or Inhibiting?

We often contemplate team dynamics in start-ups and muse over the roles and importance of employees as part of the people process. We sometimes, tend to overlook a very crucial aspect – leading from the center!

The core of a partnership start-up, is knit with partnerships. These like any other relationships may either further the purpose or impede and undo the plans and objectives.

I for one, unequivocally believe that partnerships are good for start-ups since being the number one in an organization carries the inherent risk of loneliness. "It is undoubtedly lonely at the top."

The right business partnership between the right people can enhance the ethos of a start-up. A strong partnership offers a well of resources, knowledge, expertise and a bouncing board of ideas which one has access to.

If one were to take a dispassionate view of start-up partnerships, the pros and cons of it would be revealed. The pros are immense.

Relationships are real value drivers and this manifests itself extremely poignantly in start-up partnerships. If there is a collaborative win-win mentality with forward thinking, then that is one of the most unique advantages. Partnerships must be viewed through an altruistic lens. The main objective should be to grow and prosper together.

As for the cons, yes, they do exist and interactions may give way to altercations, but if rejections are handled with expertise, then the door is left open for future connections, mutual support and companionship.

I discovered that in real time start-ups the dividing line between the pros and cons is not distinct. In fact, the initial stages of partnership are misleading. You start off with only the pros and then during the journey the cons start emerging.

My partnership engagement objective was to enrich my start-ups with different perspectives foussed on a single goal. Partners carry their own unique experiences and expertise. If one partner is well versed with financial knowledge and the other is more of a people skills person then that combination enriches the start-up. Energies derived from both, can be channelised in different directions for the company to emerge as a multi-dimensional conglomerate.

As I dwell on my initial partnership venture, my Edu-Tech Company, I realize that my partnership started off with minimal interference from my partner. He already had his hands full with other projects, hence this was more of a hobby and indulgence. I very soon realized that we were not in it together. He was focused on the revenue and he had scant interest in the highs and lows that we were experiencing. For me, it was my life line. Its success was crucial to my existence. I had given my heart and soul to it. The stark difference was in our degree of involvement. The minimal interference that I looked upon as a pro giving me the free hand and liberty to direct the working of the company in a way that I deemed fit, eventually turned out to be a con because I had nobody to share my ideas with. I had nobody to support me in decisions and in times of failure, I had nobody to talk to about the next strategy.

In my wellness start-up, the partnership scenario was a bit different. We started off together with a common objective of creating a fitness revolution in the industry and creating a profitable venture. It was smooth sailing initially and what looked as an impeccable partnership started showing signs of cracks and differences.

There were arguments, that were unresolved, there came about an arrogance merely because of the higher stakes my partner had. The beginning of the end was very soon signalled. What had started off as a common objective started dwindling away as a failed venture. The final blow was dealt by a strong wave of nepotism.

Being a bigger stake holder and a bigger investor, my partner started permitting his family members to make inroads into our daily work. Not being qualified enough to understand the functioning and strategy, their suggestions and style of working was absolutely misplaced. The newly inducted management team members had the backing of my partner with a financial clout, but lacked the professional skills to take the company ahead. Differences of opinion and lack of expertise saw the crumbling of the very foundation of the start-up and it was then that I determined to exercise my option.

I planned my timely exit by selling my stakes while the company was still profitable. I moved out at an opportune time.

The bane of nepotism introduces you to the numerous members in your partners' family who suddenly spring up as heir apparent and decide to have their say in the daily proceedings of the company. I can still remember my shock when I saw the young nephew of my partner breeze into our Board meeting and place himself very comfortably in a chair. As if this was nothing out of the ordinary and just a done thing, my partner Naveen just introduced him as a new addition to the management team. My incredulous look, my open-mouthed expression were promptly dismissed.

The 23-year old Shakun wore a smug expression as he looked at me. This expression stemmed from his closeness to his uncle. He had apparently been told that any resistance to his appointment was inconsequential. He was backed by the financial clout of his uncle's investment. As for Naveen, he did not think it wise enough to discuss this appointment with me, his partnership was rooted in his objective of profit making, which he felt this young modern boy full of new ideas would be able to swing effectively. Naveen did not care about relationships as I learnt to my dismay. Unable to invest time in this start-up he had made room for his relative to keep that vigilant eye on his investment and hopefully take it to generate more.

Successors like Shakun, sailing on a cloud of nepotism, lack the necessary skills and acumen. Regretfully though, they are invested with the power to question and if I may say the power to meddle and create chaos.

A new realization dawned with this move of mine. I realized that irrespective of the fate of partnerships an entrepreneur must have his antenna tuned to interpret the frequencies and signals of failures and successes during the start-up journey. If a partnership is not working out, then rather than let it carry on and impact everybody involved in it negatively, an exit plan must be in place. You must be armed with your strategies of either letting go if it is not yielding good results as planned or letting go if it has registered a profit and your role is more or less over. Carrying on just for attachment sake heralds doom, both for you and the organization. For successful entrepreneur's I would propagate a "detached attachment."

I have looked within. and come up with a wealth of knowledge accumulated over the years. I, like many others have always been charmed by partnerships in a start-up. A free flow of ideas, agreeing to disagree, imbibing different perspectives and views, learning to cope with different work styles, having a deeper pool of cash and resources, and many more advantages lure entrepreneur's towards establishing partnerships.

But as I learned, during my tryst with start-ups, even when partnerships start off well, the journey ahead is dotted with numerous risks and disadvantages. Some partnerships dwindle owing to a lackadaisical attitude, as the involvement and interest of one partner is not strong enough to propel the start-up ahead or help it survive against all odds. Even if the company is performing well, the joy of sharing and growing is not participative. It becomes one sided. The very essence of a partnership is defeated.

Another fate that partnerships meet is failure, because they become combative. The partner if he happens to be a larger stakeholder and bigger investor, quite mistakenly assumes the role of the boss. The meetings become breeding grounds where conflicts arise. Every partner becomes the Chief. Thus begin a series of arm-twisting meetings and interactions where getting the better of the other partner tops the agenda. The arguments are just for the sake of arguments, defying any purpose or logic.

Important and crucial decisions cannot be taken as the top management can't look beyond ego clashes to come to a mutually agreeable solution. There prevails a constant tussle between the more assertive partner and the lesser one.

One of the biggest challenges in partnerships is to find a common meeting ground on many occasions. Relationships evolve and change over the years. The key to a good partnership is also to know when to call it a day. For the general health and wellbeing of the company, it is best to sever partnerships that are not working. And make that timely exit.

Most of the partnerships that are formed with good intentions fail owing to a variety of reasons, most of which are preventable.

Start-up partnerships are inviting and alluring but only for those who can handle its intricacies – partnerships are not meant for all entrepreneur's as they are labelled " Handle With Care!"

14 Start-up Failures Are Inevitable but so Is Learning!

The bittersweet truth of start-ups is that most of them fail and very few succeed. The entrepreneurial ecosystem is replete with failures. Some entrepreneur's display it in start-up circles as a rite to passage and as an inseparable part of their start-up journey. Some entrepreneur's even flaunt it as a badge of honour. There are others who never admit the failure and attribute the winding up to other pressing needs in business and their lack of time to attend to the new venture.

I shall do neither. I shall meticulously lay the bare facts and attempt an analysis of the events in their chronological order.

As the founder of a healthy vegetarian dessert start-up, I was teeming with enthusiasm and the desire to take the industry by storm. We had a brilliant hitherto unexplored concept for the Indian market. We were optimistic that we would capture a large part of the dessert market by encashing on the vegetarianism aspect, given that a large part of the Indian population was vegetarian. I was driven by the motto of giving consumers what they wanted, or so I thought!

This very premise on which I started was to be my undoing, as I later discovered.

We went ahead and launched our unique healthy vegetarian dessert and met with early success. The curiosity factor of consumers was what gave us the much welcome nudge into the market. We targeted malls for our outlets and very soon we had 20 such outlets. We opted for the franchisee model and went on a signing spree with a good number of franchisees and a handsome amount as franchisee fees in our kitty.

The next step was to hire competent staff, we hired employees on high salaries since our early financial success had adequate, even surplus funds at that stage. We were on a no compromise employee hiring tizzy, and spared no efforts in hiring the best.

The natural corollary of this was to consider expansion. Expansion is often regarded as a good measure of success and bears testimony to the standing of a company. We were even considering the option of expanding beyond our geographical boundaries-

overseas. For the time being we were content flying in sous chefs from the best 5-star luxury chains in India to various locations.

So busy were my partners and me in this herculean addictive expansion exercise that we failed to notice the initial dip in sales. We failed to pay heed to the fact, that while we were busy focusing on new franchisees, the old ones were failing us. In order to survive in the fast-dwindling market of consumer tastes, the franchise owners were cutting corners to save costs. This was impacting the quality of the product. They had stopped adhering to the rule books handed out by us and were even altering the recipe and ingredients. We were probably aware of this in some deep dark corner of our minds, but did not want this knowledge to surface into a confrontation with them. We were guilty by self-admission of turning a blind eye at that stage. The volume of customer complaints grew and revenue started dipping as steeply as it had risen initially. We were spending so much time on creating an empire, acquiring franchisees that we completely overlooked the customer preferences and our priority to adapt to those.

A sales review meeting with Shrikant, our Sales Head bypassed the wake-up call and led to a blame game of our competitors. Shrikant mentioned some new entrants and how pricing was being used to usurp our market share. He was of the firm opinion that the customer complaints were all planted by competition and in fact we just needed more franchisees and expansion. The geographical growth of the company as well as an increase in the number of outlets would be a befitting reply to our competitors. Sometimes people are willingly gullible and walk into well laid out traps just as we did then. Our major expansion spree done, high-cost employees hired and sales at an all time low.

The subsequent Board meetings centered around more investment in the company. Everybody in the senior management team was unanimous that more money needed to be pumped in. This was a vehement suggestion by all, but there was no follow up action. Neither the promoters nor the partners, were willing to invest. The common proposition, had no takers!

The weight of the top-heavy company and accruing debts and unpaid salaries left us finally with no option but to shut shop. Not only did the business die an untimely death but all our aspirations, dreams and optimism too suffocated and collapsed.

This was indeed a failed start-up!

I am of the firm opinion that a post-mortem of all

failures is crucial to success and one's bouncing back in business! And that's what I did, both the analysis and the back in action bit.

So, what were the pearls of wisdom that I enriched myself with?

I, like most entrepreneur's was consumed by a burning desire to create a world changing impact based on my "gut feel" of success. I learned that assumptions and presumptions without the backing of a market research on consumer behavior and a product-market fit, inevitably carry the seeds of failure.

A post-mortem of the importance of being passionate revealed that passion is acceptable as long as it doesn't give way to overconfidence. Mine resulted in a penchant to skip the critical upfront customer research. So blinded was I, with the string of franchisees knocking at our door and the ringing of the cash registers that customer needs took a back seat.

My reflections on hiring the costliest talent – resulted in instilling an awareness that creation of a rock-solid foundation for an organization or company should be the prime focus. That itself should be a talent magnet. The bait of high salaries is ephemeral and once the company incurs losses, those very salaries become a death trap for the owners. The discerning highly paid employees too, don't last in the wake of a no salary or delayed salary scenario and make a hasty exit, leaving those coveted seats of power vacant. High attrition levels and that too in senior positions are detrimental for any company as it impacts the daily functioning of the business.

The grouse of no promoter or investor backing gave way to my learning that start-ups need to be frugal and investors are wary of sinking ships.

The ability to understand when to cut your losses and redirect efforts and funds elsewhere is crucial. Money is a finite source and therefore judicious allocation is the need of the hour. Floundering and clinging on to a straw of monetary resources is a definite no no.

A few other reasons for the failure of start-ups that emerged were –

The reluctance to admit the product-market misfit well in time. Being married to a bad idea, or a product or even a bad underperforming employee is the pitfall of many businesses.

The key to remaining a successful entrepreneur is to know when you have to make a clean razor-sharp cut and sever the businesses that are not performing.

Preparedness and maturity to face the initial

consequences of a start-up journey are also very important. My partners and I were so attached to an idea that we thought was so unique that we were unwilling to let go. We brushed the early warning signs under the carpet. We did not realize that health and desserts do not go down well in the Indian consumer psyche. Desserts had to be the sinful cravings that would satiate those with a sweet tooth. The initial customer curiosity was short lived and we should have permitted its' "sweet" death.

We also learned that involving investors right from the beginning is of utmost importance. Just putting up a brave front to show that all is well and then suddenly springing a surprise asking for investments is unwise and doesn't fetch any results. The franchisee model of pricing products is a dark art that reflects sharply in a start-up success. The products need to be priced high enough to cover costs, yet should be low enough to attract customers.

Another hazard faced by start-ups which fortunately did not impact us is legal complexities. This can happen when your idea enters a legal mess and for want of any better solution, has to be closed.

We often hear that pivoting is good, but in my opinion, unless pivoting has a purpose it is nonproductive. Changes to a business model, should be made when needed. The testing of hypotheses and measuring of results also becomes imperative.

An unavoidable corollary of failed start-ups is the discord between partners. If they are existing friends who have formed a partnership then the loss is two-fold – you lose a business partner and you also strain friendships. Being human and possessing emotions is something that is best seen in the arena of a failed start-up, where raw emotions are on display. The gamut spans – guilt, anger, sadness, shame, resentment et all. When dreams are dashed and self-confidence shattered, it is a herculean task to maintain a brave façade. If truth be told - at ground zero it hurts!

Handling business partnerships needs maturity and resilience.

Another peculiar characteristic of failed start-ups is scapegoating. The obvious targets are either the founders/partners or then the rivals and competition who are blamed for outsmarting them. During the post-mortem of my failed start-up I realized, that if anybody was to be blamed, it was me and my team. This knowledge was to pave the way for my future successes because I realized that the "buck must stop with me."

I smiled to myself as I reflected on my failed start-up, gone were the feelings of despair and remorse. I could feel a new surge of emotions, a new vitality, a new source of energy, beckoning me to newer frontiers. I had learned many valuable lessons from this debacle. I was transformed, enlightened and armed with the power of my knowledge.

I moved out of my cabin and shut the door behind me, almost symbolic of shutting out the failure in the past and moving towards new beginnings.

As I bent forward to push the door open in front of me, I could read the bold, clear and unwritten message on it, which was to be my greatest learning – "Before success comes failure!"

15 Options, Decisions and Reflections.......

The popular cliché of life is a journey with a myriad options and one has to choose from what is on offer, never rang true for me. I am a firm advocator of the fact that one has to create their own options and alter course with a slight turn of the wheel as and when needed during the journey.

The power of recasting your destiny with new circumstances, events and choices rests in your alacrity and wisdom. It is important to understand that our choices and decisions need not be perfect, we are entitled to herald failure and defeat too. There are numerous opportunities for countless indecisions, visions, revisions. It is akin to drawing out cards, you must know which one will improve your game. You must have the swiftness and quick thinking to discard the weaker cards and pick out the stronger ones, before the entire deck has been played. It is our choices and decisions that shape our lives and therefore it is rightly said that we are the creators of our destiny.

My early life was devoid of multiple choices. I came from a financially weak background, where schooling was an option but not the choice of school. I enrolled in a Malayalam medium school. As a child I was not aware that dreams have to be restricted to the options available, hence I dreamt of big things, and opportunities which were not visible through the lens of my school education. I dreamt of a career in investment banking and moving to big cities for my college education and work.

The first big realization that dawned upon me was that the world outside my Malayalam medium comfort zone, was driven by an alien super power which people called English. This was the prevalent language for communication and had a tyrannical dominance in all things big or small. It ruled conversations, it ruled your writing, it was your badge of honour for job applications, deciding on your acceptance in friend circles and groups, in short you had no future if you did not know English. Time to take the bull by the horns and I embarked on what seemed like mission impossible – befriending the English language! A slight turn of the wheel, a change of course. Gruelling training sessions, watching English movies and serials, conversing with those who were well versed with the language and presto - I was English ready!

I joined a prestigious college in New Delhi, for my graduation. My love for public speaking and mastery of the alien language made me a well-known public speaker. Participating and winning in college debates, extempore speeches came easily and effortlessly for me.

Influenced by my parents and their wishes I started a career in accounting with a heart set on capital markets. Physically I was on my seat and churning out routine work but not mentally. I kept the momentum and wheel of my career rolling by making my moves from accounts to finance then consulting, but the pace was missing there was no exhilaration! My heart and passion were elsewhere—the Capital market!

As my inner calling grew more distinct and louder, I realized that the time to turn the wheel had come once again. Investment Banking was my next choice and I felt the pace of my career take a jump-start. The reputed company that I joined was the industry leader. It was a dream job on several counts for me. I had a senior designation, a job that I enjoyed doing and it had a lot of perks.

The plush office brought along with it a matching travel and lifestyle. I was flying first or business class on my official tours, staying in the luxury five-star chains and generally living the enviable life of a business tycoon without owing the business.

I remember the day that I had to leave for a business trip to Delhi and a luxury car was waiting for me to bundle in my suitcases and set off. I felt the stirrings of a very unfamiliar emotion. Not being able to pinpoint what it was, and also being very short of time; I did not mull over it but went about my routine activity of donning my suit and tie for the flight since the business meeting that was lined up would not give me enough time to change at the hotel. My hands felt as if there were dead-weights attached to the wrists and just would not move fast. Why was I unable to complete a task that in the past was so exciting that it would take me a few minutes only? I had a business class ticket, a luxury car waiting downstairs and 3 days stay in a five-star luxury hotel, wasn't that incentive enough to move fast and board that flight? Hadn't I always dreamt of this life? So, then what was it? Unable to find an answer despite internal probing I resigned myself to the task on hand and completed it albeit a little behind schedule.

Boarding card in hand I made my way to the airport lounge and took care to enter the area marked "Gold/ Platinum customers only." After years of jet setting for business meetings in first and business class I had earned the distinction of a high-end, well respected and valued VIP frequent flyer.

Deciding to appease the feeling of emptiness in my stomach, I made my way to the well laid out breakfast table. The carefully planned and well-presented spread was a visual treat. The scones, sandwiches, non-vegetarian dishes, English breakfast, Indian delectable cuisine, were yours for the taking and offered an unparalleled joy to the foodies and their taste buds. Why was it then that the same deadweight feeling resurfaced? The emptiness and hollow feeling in my stomach grew stronger. Had it nothing to do with hunger? Was I ill? Why did the aroma of the food fail to tempt me?

This time the introspection came up with a startling result, I could promptly identify the hollow feeling in my stomach and its accompanying emotion – boredom! Yes, I was bored of my extravagant life style, I was bored of living out of suitcases, I was bored of nodding my head, acknowledging and saying thank you for the numerous VIP courtesies that were rendered to me as part of my travel. I was fed up of moving from one meeting to another, representing my company, documenting my discussions, reporting and lining up yet another meeting, yet another travel, yet another business destination. My life had become a very smooth predictable circle. I now craved for the jagged edges, the uncertainties, the options and choices of exploring beyond what was handed over to me.

I wanted the liberty to experiment, to create, to feel the rush of adrenaline which my cushioned and comfortable work life style was not giving me. Yes, there were uncertainties, from one business meeting to another. Sometime things did not go my way, but those challenges were surmountable and did not sap my passion, they did not infuse me with thrill and excitement.

This was the hunger and emptiness I felt in my stomach that could not be satiated with food and my current job. I had had an over indulgence of 22 years of gorging on a career and lifestyle that took me to VP, and CEO levels, it was time to diet and slim down and shed off the extra kilos of unwanted career perks. I decided to change course once again, this time the steering wheel had to be turned almost full circle and stop at where I had started my career – level zero!

When I walked into office next, my mind was made up. I was enveloped with a new spirit of adventure, the thrill of starting afresh. Customary greetings exchanged, regular instructions and work attended to and I was ready to break the news to my Chairman. Finding a suitable opportunity, I entered his cabin and voila it was done! Well from my side it was, but judging from his expression, (he still seemed to be reeling under the aftermath of the news) I was pretty sure that from his end it was far from over.

"So, GR may I ask you what has prompted you to take this decision?" I must have made no sense to him and looked quite foolish and cut a rather sorry figure when I said I just wanted to be unshackled and left free to experiment. I was a perfect candidate for being reprimanded as an errant child at that moment, because I had voiced this unpalatable desire to a man who was the ultimate representation of what shackles of power and position could do. He was sitting on the topmost coveted rung of the ladder. Would he appreciate my viewpoint? Nah ... that was wishful thinking.

Still trying to brave his incredulous look, I repeated what I had said earlier hoping that it would sink in as my final decision, A wave of his hand signalling me to the door saying that he would think about it and let me know by tomorrow on the way forward, ended the revelatory meeting. People leaving in senior positions comes with its own set of complications and I was perfectly aware of that.

Deliberations, discussions, opinions, cautionary advice, warnings, all died a natural death when faced with my headstrong resolve. I had all these years climbed the rungs of the corporate ladder sometimes slowly sometimes fast but taking care not to misjudge a step or fall off, and then at the point of deliverance I discovered that the ladder I was climbing so relentlessly and carefully all these years was resting on the wrong wall! But being me, and knowing that I had to create my own options, I changed course yet again, by moving the ladder to another wall!

Most of us grapple with the options on offer, trying to make the most of those. We sweat, we toil, we fail to experiment content and cushioned in our small world of achievements and successes. We do not have the vision or courage to stretch out our hands and grab other invisible options or choices that may have the potential of turning out to be better.

One does not have to dedicate one's work life to what somebody else offers us, life offers us the chance to create our own options, decisions and follow it up with reflections. Weigh your choices, seek newer options till you know which is the best. I was on my way to doing just that!

"Ah, but a man's reach must exceed his grasp or what's a heaven for?"

A month later I was metaphorically set free, with a song in my heart and a spring in my step........... come join me as I enter the second innings of my career ....

16 Trading My Shiny Corporate Shoes for a Pair of Sneakers—Sprint Ready on New Turf!

The evening setting sun on the distant horizon still shining brightly almost blinding me with its brilliance, was the subject of my rumination as I sat in my plush Cuffe Parade apartment balcony. This fire ball of glory, appeared every morning, unquestioningly, dedicatedly, illuminating and infusing everything around it with its warmth, signalling a fresh start to the day and then bidding adieu to rise again the next day. My career at that point of time oddly felt similar. I too had followed this predictable pattern of a cyclical routine.

My mind was a cluttered space of thoughts and emotions. I had to sift through to pick the dominant one and presto - there it was. It was the drive for adventure, the desire to explore. It was almost as if the spirit of Columbus was beckoning me on an exploratory mission of the dark and unknown expanse where the rays of this warm sun did not penetrate. Unlike Christopher Columbus and his legendary ships on the voyage I was equipped with the beacon of my experience and knowledge to guide me through my journey and light up the path ahead. We however, shared one common goal – the mission of reaching our respective destinations through the passion for discovery!

The next day arrived and it was time for me to dress up for my part – yes, I had to mirror the same enthusiasm I felt within, through my sparkling clean and well ironed clothes and smart appearance.

I had to accessorise my look with a dash of histrionics. A loud good morning, a swift movement to reach out for the morning newspaper, cracking a rather unappealing joke on the breakfast served by the cook. My shoddy attempt to slice a piece of "upma" with a knife, which looked like a well decorated cake, while singing a Happy Birthday song drew no smiles from the expressionless faces around me. A few close family members other than my wife and daughter, were not happy with my decision, they saw no merit in me having worked my way up the corporate ladder only to kick the ladder and land with my feet on the ground and start walking once again. The fact that I had chosen to leave my comfortable 9 -5 job at the very zenith of my career and land at ground zero with a looming and big question mark on the work horizon was something truly beyond their comprehension. Their only way of revolting was a no response, silent encounter with me. When I had broken the news to them the previous evening, they had tried to reason and argue it out with me but had eventually reconciled to the situation as they saw they were not making any headway. I do not blame them, for how could they measure the depth of my enthusiasm? there was no way they could peep into the realms of my mind to see the zillion exciting thoughts that it was harbouring about my work in future.

I left home at my usual office time, for a moment trying to cheat myself about the fact that I was actually going to office. I pretended to forget that I had no timing to adhere to on that day. Once in the car, all pretensions dropped, I had no clue of where I wanted to go. I drove a few kilometres ahead of my house, and parked in a quiet corner, thinking about my future plan. I came up with a few names from my business contact list whom I would call on and discuss the way forward. I had a "gut feel" that they would be the right bouncing boards for my idea and luck, good counsel and reasoning prevailing would team up with me on my start-up ventures.

The first telephone call was made and my appointment lined up. The thought that I had my first meeting lined up for my very own future start-up was so thrilling by itself that I was enveloped with an adrenaline rush.

Our meeting lasted a good 4 hours and I walked out with a bag of mixed feelings. No commitments, no conclusions but yet there was a glimmer of hope. Planning for the future had at least started off on the right note. I had the first half tick on my bucket list – that although didn't indicate the full attainment of my wish it at least signalled my working towards its fulfilment.

Next on my agenda was lunch and stopping at the coffee shop of a popular 5-star hotel on the way, which was a part of my old routine. I had no intention of giving up my previous lifestyle. I was comfortable financially and that had served as a cushion for my impulsive and rash decision to quit the corporate world. Financial independence had indeed played a very crucial role in my decision-making process. Coming from a financial background with a keen and expert eye on finances it would have been a big disaster if I had failed on that account. I had a carefully developed inflation proof cash flow statement in mind with an optimistically calculated life span of 90 years. With a no compromises kind of lifestyle, adequate health care, child's education and wedding expenses and other needs factored in. I had left no room for disenchantment on the financial front had my future ventures failed.

Half way through my meal, I tried to justify to myself why I had quit. My mind went back to that day at work, when I had finally decided to move on sans my job and its perks. It was probably one of my busiest days at work and suddenly mid-way I had called my assistant to inform her to postpone my engagements and meetings for the rest of the day. I was so overcome with a niggling feeling in my mind that I needed some "Me Time" to sit back and think it through. I asked myself if I was moving in the right direction, since boredom with my corporate routine had set in so strongly. I asked myself a couple of valid questions:

Was I truly enjoying my work? Pat came the answer NO!

Was I investing enough time on my passions and interests other than the desire to ace my current job? Was I giving enough time to my family? (I had missed out on the growing up years of my daughter I was so preoccupied with work and travel that I was hardly home.) The answer was a foregone conclusion. It was a big NO.

Hence my decision of quitting was the only option I had. Justification given, my mind at rest and the remainder of the lunch was dealt with.

I moved on to my next meeting. The same round of animated discussions, the same non-committal conclusions yet a distinct and strong ray of hope.

Ironically though with no conclusion in sight, no concrete plans for the next day, as I headed home, I had a bounce in my steps and a feeling of having worked the entire day. I did not have to take recourse to any play acting when I was seated with my family at the dinner table, the confidence and elation that I felt at that time, came from within.

I adopted the same modus operandi for the next few months and then finally the glimmer of hope developed into a strong light that illuminated my future work path with its bright shine.

Very soon I was the co-founder of not 1 but 4 start-ups! A document storage company, a wellness start-up, a computer training company and one in the financial sector – trading and stock broking.

All entrepreneur's have their individual traits and characteristics and my predominant ones were being sector agnostic, having multiple start-ups and always creating companies with partnerships – never being the sole owner.

Confidence is a precious lifeboat you have, when you set sail on the unchartered oceans of entrepreneurship. I too had mine inflated and ready to use when I ran into unexpected rough weather. I was very confident that with my multi-skilled persona and expertise

I would definitely not sink into the deep dark ocean of uncertainty. I believed in hedging my risk options and from that stemmed my sector agnosticism and the basis of starting multiple companies.

I was certain that all would not be doomed even if I met with failure, and that was the simple premise that formed the basis of my second innings.

Work life went back to a routine, with objectives, goals and agendas, but this time there was a distinct difference, the goals and agendas were all mine. I was the creator not only the executor as in my corporate career. There were days of failure, days of successes, days that were uneventful and routine. The uniqueness of risks spread out in separate baskets, but the promise of profit from all the baskets was an unparalleled thrill by itself.

This feeling was so different from a unifocused corporate job. You owned the failures and the successes in totality. The sense of belonging was very pronounced.

One fine day, after a busy day at work, my close friend Harish paid me a visit. Harish asked me how my start-up experience had been and my answer was a crisp and to the point – "Heady and eventful!"

This casual question from him, set my mind ticking and unleashed a screenplay and flashback of memories.

The ensuing chapter premiers my movie titled "Dreams sprout wings -Work life after 40"– as part of my nostalgic journey and ruminations, where I play the producer, director and actor!

The movie has all the makings of a blockbuster. The critics review read Harish here, spells it all – A well-planned second innings is undoubtedly a prescription for success!

17 Reflections on the Method in My Madness....

Deviations from the set path, attempting to break away from accepted norms, experimenting, dismissing routines, jumping into the unknown, especially at the later stages of one's career are not taken well by many. I too had my fair share of discouragements, rejections, dismissals, incredulous looks to even sympathy and pity from people who genuinely thought that I was possessed or had simply "lost it."

Why would I kick up position, power, luxury and other accompanying perks to once again be a vagabond and explorer on the career landscape, was a question plaguing many - except me!

As the writer, producer and actor of my ambitious mission I had all the answers. A first hand feel of boredom, the lack of challenges, a surfeit of luxury (if ever there could be one, unbelievable yet true for me.)

The human mind is a repository of memories that never fade. One just has to delve in and pull out the relevant ones, as and when needed.

Flashback to my new career beginnings – a 40-year-old with the zeal and enthusiasm of a newbie, a man desirous of etching a mark of his design and choice on the business façade.

I had turned writer, director, producer for my upcoming blockbuster – the script was written and the rest was all set to follow.

Let's delve into my four blockbusters that defined my second innings. The wellness start-up made me an overnight star. The initial teething problems over, and we were well on our way to a meteoric rise and success. Apart from the misjudgement and miscalculation of trying to introduce self-defense techniques for women and the health juices initiative to my captive gym audience, that failed big time, the passion, dedication and innovation that the entire canvas of this venture was painted with, left me one happy man!

My document storage company taught me how the initial desperation in start-ups to win big accounts and names can become a cliff hanger.

The penalty clause which I added on an impulse for defaulting on timely deliveries did not make rational business sense, but quite ironically it proved to be the best offer I made – the deal clincher! I won the contract that proved to be the forerunner of many other big ones. It was passion and dedication that I brought to the fore that helped me wade through the uncertainties, the doubts the trials and the tribulations to emerge at the other end of the shore – confident and victorious!

My other two successful ventures – the financial company and the computer training company too saw passion and dedication form the strong impenetrable layers at the surface that trapped all failures and negativity. What lay below those layers was then pure success.

My last 20 years as an entrepreneur, founder of 4 big successful start-ups and a few failed ones, has overall been rewarding and enriching. Although the successes outnumbered the failures there was no denying that they were both two sides of the same coin. Both co-existed. It is for you to toss the coin and deal with the side that faces you. If you have the wrong side facing you- flip if back again!

When failure faced me, it sapped me of my enthusiasm, my optimism my courage, and all positivity, till I decided to toss the coin again.

All my success start-up stories had a few key elements ingrained in them –

The first one was to do things with passion or not at all. All the companies that I founded and that were successful are either 1,2, or 3 in the industry. I strongly believe that being a market leader or at least in the first three ranks is imperative. A start-up cannot be mediocre. It has to be your labour of love, watered by your passion and dedication.

My second belief is that after you have set up a successful company and if you are exiting for any reason be very certain that you will not venture into the same field again. The reason being that one cannot recreate the same magnum opus. Blockbusters in specific industries are produced only once. It will be difficult to compete with the phenomenal success of your very own first creation. You would never want one sibling to outperform the other.

My third learning was one which I have pointed out earlier too. One must have a "detached attachment "with all their ventures. The cling on style of functioning will be counterproductive. If your start-up has reached the zenith of its success and your role as the actor is over, and your final lines delivered, then one must encash on their commercials and move on.

In the contrasting situation of failed start-ups where you know that you are aboard a sinking ship and the hole is getting bigger and the ship will capsize very soon, you must reach out for your lifeboat. I would strongly advocate the sever and move on instead of a cling on and hope for recovery approach.

The fourth aspect which I adopted was being sector agnostic and adopting multiple start-ups at a time. I knew that most start-ups fail not because of the entrepreneur but because of extraneous circumstances which are beyond our control. Having your risks mitigated and interests and efforts divided will cushion the blow of failed ventures. Single ventures run very high risks.

The fifth important aspect which I have also mentioned earlier is embarking on partnership ventures. There is power in numbers. You may call it financial power, emotional power, the power of harnessing expertise or something else. I would very simply define it as the power of sharing! You have your joys, successes, failures, apprehensions and many more emotions which feel better when shared.

The last most important learning is to be prepared for all eventualities. When you walk in you do it with your eyes wide open. It is not difficult to understand that the journey ahead is long, terrifying at times, exhausting, exhilarating, but ultimately rewarding.

One must be prepared to give that proverbial pound of flesh to gain the rewards of success.

A commitment to your vision and a sense of purpose is what is imperative to move the needle forward.

Entrepreneurship is immensely rewarding but is high risk prone. Most businesses fail, entrepreneur's suffer burn outs and fade out.

One must as an entrepreneur list out their fears related to a fresh start and as they move on, start conquering them one by one.

When I decided to write my own script, produce my own movie and be the lead actor, it was a freefall that I opted for with my eyes wide open. I could see the dangerous yet alluring topography below me. I could see the cliffs and the ravines I had to avoid. I could see the plateau that beckoned me temptingly. I knew that I should not fall prey to resting on that as that would mean pausing and applying a break on my exciting journey.

I had to stay focused on my flight ahead. I conquered new peaks. I played many parts, I took on whatever roles came my way, - I was the HR manager hiring employees, I was the sales manager making presentations to clients, I was the CEO assuming responsibilities and taking on a leadership role when called for, I was the enviable 'all in one' Man Friday.

While surveying the landscape of my new territory I knew that I had another destination I could veer towards – my retired life! It was true that I had given up big bucks, my designation and luxurious lifestyle, but I had amassed enough which although would not be replenished, was at least a strong cushion against the future odds. The comforts of my family were taken care of. This foresight while making a fresh start is something I would strongly advocate. Let your risks not prove disastrous for your near and dear ones who are dependent on you.

I had therefore, created the safe territory earlier in my career. I had financial comfort and backing which I could always head back to if I failed. Most importantly, I had a plan and the power of a parachute with me. It would I was sure prevent me from a headfirst fall on the start-up ground.

In my second innings I did not focus on the fear. I had the parachute of passion and dedication well strapped on to my body when I made the plunge.

I can still feel the thrill of adventure as I sky dived and cruised over the new landscape, having relegated fear to the dark recesses of my mind. The primary thoughts on my mind were focused on safe landing and displaying the proverbial flag of achievements. Enthusiasm, passion, dedication were all fueled in good measure and were never in short supply.

I flew past many entrepreneur's who were hurtling down with great force owing to their failed ventures.

With 4 multi-bagger blockbusters and 5 mega ventures, I had indeed achieved the feat of etching the magical number 9 to the individual success stories pillar that stood tall in the business world.

A profound realization dawned upon me when I was concluding my film in my mind's eye of my 20 years start-up journey.

I was engulfed with the sharp and welcome realization that when I had reached out for my parachute mid-air, it had OPENED and I had had a perfectly smooth landing!

18

Rummaging Through the Hat of Experience and Pulling Out the Critical Success Factors for Start-ups.

The daily routine of going through my mail just before I went to bed, one evening led me to an unread message from a premier management institute. It was an invitation to address their final year students. I was invited in the capacity of a successful serial entrepreneur to add a zing to their new innings as they forayed into the business world.

While typing out a short acceptance email, I realized that I had a very responsible task to perform. I would probably have to nudge out the blinkers that some of them would be wearing, I would probably have to shine the bright light of wisdom on the dark and cluttered mindscape of a few, or probably just give a slight push in the right direction to those with their wings open and the potential to soar.

As I retired for the night, sleep evaded me. This mail was a trigger that unleashed a million thoughts in my mind. All of us wear an invisible hat – the hat of experience. I reached out for mine, that night, desirous of going through its contents.

I was quickly transported to the day I decided to quit my steady job and its accompanying luxuries. The day I walked into my regular 5 Star hotel for a cup of tea, after quitting, devoid of my previous designation of the CEO of a reputed company. That day, I was met by the hotel's Director of Sales—Mr Goel, who greeted me enthusiastically. Half way through my cup of tea and the snacks that had been so generously ordered by Mr Goel, I broke the news to him about my new venture and how I no longer represented my previous company. I was amazed at the alacrity at which he decided to rush for a sales review meeting. What surprised me even more was the bill that was brought to me for the snacks which had been ordered by him for me. This was to set the precedent for more such incidents.

I remember meeting the CEO of a company, a peer of mine, at the Royal Western Turf Club, during the racing season. Our customary handshakes over, and pleasantries exchanged, I expressed my desire to meet him in his office the next day. I had him on my mind as a potential investor for my upcoming start-up. An effusive nod of the head and "anytime my friend, just give me a call with an hour's notice and just drop in" was the usual way we saw and met each other, so nothing out of the ordinary in that. However, what ensued immediately thereafter, was the staggering truth and reality that was to stay with me in my initial start-up journey. Upon being asked the agenda of the meeting, I informed him about my new status sans my previous job and title. The human face they say is a wonderful mirror of emotions, and not all of us are adept at hiding those. Rammy my friend was a complete failure on that score. I could see his expression change from bewilderment to shock to a questioning "Why would I want to meet you and waste my time?" kind of a look. He bid a hurried good bye to me and left. As I was preparing to get into the car, my cell phone rang. It was a call from Rammy. He had suddenly remembered that he had an important meeting the next day and then would be leaving on a tour to Delhi the day after. He also mentioned that in future I could contact his secretary to line up any appointments with him, since she knew his availability for meetings. This was his subtle severance as I soon realized, of any business contact with me.

This did come as a harsh blow to me but I admired myself at my ability to not reel under this for long. I knew I had chosen an untrodden path, where I was the lone traveller initially. My enthusiasm a wee bit dampened but my desire to prove to myself and the world that I had the flames of my passion burning high, gained stronger momentum.

Zeroing down on the critical success factors I shall attempt to list them down methodically if not chronologically.

I had started out with a few very clear concepts and a few that I imbibed through trial and error or failings and misses.

I was very clear that I would not put all my eggs in one basket. This was not only driven by the hedging my risks prudent decision, but also carried the promise of excitement. If my risks would be mitigated, I would never suffer a huge monetary set back by focusing only on one venture. Added to this advantage would be the thrill and excitement of dabbling with various colours on my new canvas. I could experiment with different ventures that were in different fields and would never suffer monotony. When an entrepreneur suffers monotony, it kills the enthusiasm and eventually sounds the death knell of a venture.

I took a mental stock of my different ventures. Document storage company, computer training company, financial trading and stock broking, retail juices and desserts, spa, wellness, and many more, each one so different and yet so satisfying.

Engaging in different ventures considerably diminishes financial risks and adds the much-needed spirit of novelty that prevents an entrepreneur from falling into the death trap of monotony.

The other thing that was crystal clear in my mind was that whatever venture I set up successfully, I would not set up its sibling. I would strive to make it the market leader featuring in the first three ranks. That industry would be a onetime entry for me. The reason was simple. A start-up is called a start-up for a reason. One cannot have a restart of a same industry start-up. If I set up a company in the wellness industry, and it ranks as a number one, I cannot create another number one, without pushing my previous efforts down to a number two. I did not want to set up ventures one at the cost of another. The danger of benchmarking against the previous market leader that you have created also looms large on the horizon. The thrill and excitement that entrepreneur's need for start-ups would also be missing if one had to rebuild a similar company. The been there, done it all, seen it all, tried it all would then hold true.

You cannot vie to achieve the numero uno position in the same industry, without pulling down your previous labour of love!

As a corollary to this point, I would also like to mention that there are "no big comebacks" after an industry hiatus. If I were to give you a simple relatable, layman's example, superstars in Bollywood after they stop acting for a while can never become superstars again. They would have been replaced by another star who would have worked his or her way to the top.

In a very candid confession of mine I would say that all the major successes that I created in the 2000's cannot be replicated today. The times have changed, the customers have changed, many other factors both in the external and the internal environment have changed. If one were to adopt the same methodology as in the past, it would be a massive failure. For those who would have no option but to re venture, then research, upgradation of skills and knowledge, along with the ability to adapt would have to be the major driving force. I would maintain my stance that -

Returning after a business hiatus with the desire to recreate history is either minimal or largely unsuccessful!

Another thing that irks me is cash burn. A start-up is not your passport to losses. Ventures must be carefully planned to reach break evens and then get on to the road of profit. If the business is not yielding results, then winding up is the best option. Driving along in a car that is malfunctioning will not take you to your destination. You try and salvage the situation by looking for alterative ways of commuting, if you do not have the resources to look at other means, then it is best to discontinue your journey there. Do not continue in the same car refueling it because the journey cannot be completed as the other parts are not functioning.

Plan your start-up journey with milestones, a start-up as most entrepreneur's mistakenly assume is not a synonym for cash burn!

Investing in people is another critical success factor. People form the backbone of a successful organization. As the world moves towards paperless offices, increased automation, dismissal of manual tasks, I maintain that people are still integral, people are still crucial. In my start-ups in the early 80's I harboured the notion that the higher the paper qualification and years of experience the better the candidate would be. All my earlier recruitments were done keeping this in mind. In my EdTech company, I remember the file of paper qualifications of my senior employees was heavier than their sales reports and revenue collected. In short, they carried such a huge baggage of their achievements in terms of experience and qualifications, that they could not look beyond that to participate in the legwork and other demands of a start-up. I was instrumental in creating top-heavy organizations.

People are not commodities to be displayed, their capabilities should be the deciding factor in the hiring process. Investing in the right employees forms a firm stepping stone on the path of a company's road to success.

Feeling a little drained out by then with this rather thought-provoking exercise of my experience and learning and with the intention of catching up on some sleep I decided to call it a night. My hat of experiences was far from empty, it still had some very poignant take aways.

Read on, as I delve into my musings ....

19

Fixing the Remaining Pieces of the Start-up Puzzle to Complete the Picture!

Pondering over a few more interesting pieces of the critical success factors from my previous chain of thoughts, uncovered crucial aspects. I was intrigued by the hullabaloo over a start-up idea, and why entrepreneur's thought they had struck gold with it. Given that ideas germinated in the fertile thought process bed of a start-up, yet ideas by themselves did not guarantee the plant of success. Its implementation at the right time signalled the blossoming of the start-up tree.

The basic premise of an idea to kick start your venture is its uniqueness. An idea has to be unique. You may then try to zero down upon it as good or bad. A few interesting thoughts come to my mind which are worth sharing.

If you have an idea that you feel is safe, tried, tested and good, it runs the inherent risk of like-minded people chasing it. The chances of differentiation are therefore nullified or considerably diminished. The spirit of competition too, is ruled out since you can't compete with the same existing idea. On the other hand, when entrepreneur's come up with ideas that have never seen the light of day, seem to be bad ideas because they are risky, or because of their newness, they discover an insight before the others. They gain one of the greatest advantages – the competitive advantage of time.

Once you introduce the idea and initiate your start-up, by the time the others realize its existence, you are already well entrenched into the system. You become the first mover and build a momentum that makes it very difficult for others to dislodge you.

This is where timing emerges as a critical factor for success.

A unique idea launched at an opportune time is crucial.

Coupled with your unique idea should be a market research. Your product or service must have the right demand in the market. Entrepreneur's are so bowled over with their idea that they lack the astuteness of conducting adequate market research for the accompanying product or service to assess its demand. There are numerous instances of excellent ideas that failed to take off due to a lack of demand, as market research never figured in the start-up plan.

While there are many things within your control in a start-up that can be tweaked, or re tweaked, adjusted and re adjusted, the market is beyond one's control and cannot be changed. It is therefore imperative to think through your market and devote adequate time for doing so. The market for your products is the greatest predictor of your start-up's success. In a market teeming with customers, your product if well-researched, finds the perfect product-market fit. You may launch the best product with the best team of people representing it, but if there is no market, your start-up fails. You will spend precious time and years looking for non-existent customers for your products. The fantastic team that you hired with all the hand-picked people will gradually dwindle. The employees will get demoralized if the company is failing and they will be quick to desert their seats of power. This will eventually spell the doom of your start-up.

A vital aspect of market assessment and demand for your products, is not to remain focused on the current market size. You have to focus on the future market size. A10-year estimate is important. A current small market can also give you a good start, as long as it indicates a growth ahead, till at least 10 years.

A start-up product has to be part of a rapidly growing market, not necessarily a large market.

As a start-up founder, you must be willing to research the market and even going out to have a feel of the market – as a hands-on salesman. This particular point makes me reflect on how this held true for all my start-ups, but more so for my wellness one. Fitness not being a very popular or well-known concept as a business back in 2000 when I started, I decide to embark on a market research and customer potential exploratory mission.

I had no qualms in getting an actual feel of the market, so what better area for my study than the ones that the existing fitness enthusiasts frequented? The parks, the long stretch of the Marine Drive and other public places that offered ample space in the cluttered "Mayanagri" Mumbai were the ones that me along with my team targeted. My work day used to start as early as 6 am when my team members and me went and stood at strategic locations hoping to catch the eye of those who were either jogging or exercising or walking. It wasn't really difficult to do that. We carried a banana, or apple and handed it over to them subtly wrapped in paper with our gym's branding. For thc curious we gave inputs about our new gym and I can proudly say that we managed a promising number of converts from the Mumbai outdoors to our gym indoors.

Customer interaction, feedback and implementation, in the initial days creates a wonderful springboard of success!

Although, I have touched upon this earlier, I must emphasize it a wee bit more. Being dispassionate about your start-ups, helps immensely. Quite ironically, large doses of passion are needed to set up ventures in the initial days so being bereft of passion doesn't sound quite right here. Let me move on to clarify it further. Passion is crucial in the initial stages but has to be phased out, as the start-up progresses, whether on the path of success or on the path of failure.

Once your start-up scales the peaks of success and you have done your bit, you must contemplate a way of exiting. Selling off your equity and making a good return is the best and most rational option. If for some reason your venture is struggling to walk, let alone run, you must come to terms with it as a failed venture. It is best then to either shut shop or sell it off to a probable buyer and investor.

A start-up founder must cultivate the much-needed oxymoronic detached attachment with all ventures.

An analytical view of my start-up journey unearthed the important critical success factors that made them winners. I could not pinpoint on one factor but drew up a list of many that went into the pot pourri of my start-up successes!

Coming back to the analogy of the start-up jigsaw puzzle revealed that it was indeed a wonderful parallel to draw.

A start-up entrepreneur carries a bag full of a myriad shapes representing different ideas, products, plans, budgets, people and much more. The challenge that he or she faces is in placing them all together as per the available slots and completing the picture.

This puzzle is special because it is aspirational and is painted with the colours of dreams and hopes. Each individual piece is unique, since it embodies a wealth of different emotions and experiences. Sometimes you try to push pieces that are not well suited and they do not fit in. Likewise, some of your actions and ideas may not suit a particular stage of the start-up and must therefore, be readjusted and relooked at. If the pieces are not interlocking properly, it is time to discard the puzzle and look for a new one. Just as having failed in piecing together one puzzle should not prevent you from trying another one, a failed start-up too should not prevent you from launching a new one.

If you have three or four puzzles to solve together like I did, you must ensure that your attention is divided evenly across all. You need to work the puzzles with patience and determination with the objective of creating the complete picture. It takes a lot of time and effort to work the puzzles. Contrary to popular thinking, there are no short cuts to success.

Entrepreneurship in my opinion is very rewarding because it gives you the wonderful opportunity of solving the jigsaw puzzle of business. Unlike the readymade puzzles i.e., the corporate jobs, start-up puzzles don't have corners that are pre set, you have to build these corners yourself. The thrill and enthusiasm of doing this is exhilarating. Every new feature that you create during your start-up journey comes with its own new pieces and interlocking ability with another piece. Finally, all pieces lock together to deliver a clear picture.

The key to getting a good head start with the puzzle is to start building from the center. The center elucidates your core vision and the fundamental pieces should be assembled first. Your idea, product and people are a few core pieces. As you work your way outwards, you can improve the start-up by changing its design, enhancing its value, etc. Creating new pieces that interlock with the old ones can also be contemplated.

The start-up jigsaw puzzle completes the big picture of entrepreneurial efforts. What shines through is the realization that "as long as we have memories, yesterday remains and as long as we have hope, tomorrow awaits."

20 Hanging Up My Boots or Moving on? Coupling the Past With a Compelling Vision for the Future...

I for one, am averse to the word "retirement." The word brings with it a negativity that almost signals the end of life and living. I do not subscribe to the school of thought which sees a complete break from work as an oasis of solitude and happiness.

I invite you to embrace a new thought process for one of the universally accepted notions people have about work – retirement!

For a majority of us, a career is all about working up to a certain age. The options that unfold thereafter, are the well-planned drives on the lush green golf course, lazing about on sun kissed beaches, playing with grand children or other pre decided options on the well-trodden path.

Allow me to offer you an alternative view of the work future.

If peace is what retirement entails, it can be created on the busiest of days, or it can evade you on the leanest of days. It is all in the mind would be an apt way to describe this coveted emotion.

One can always create their own island of tranquility and peace wherever and whenever they want to. I remember sitting in the business class lounge at one of the busiest airports, Heathrow in London that was teeming with passengers, yet totally engrossed in the book that I was reading. I was completely oblivious to the cacophony, the clinking of glasses, spoons, forks as food was taken back and forth, so lost was I in my fictional world. It was almost as if I was alone on an island. It was only when I willed myself to come back to reality close to my boarding time, that I paid heed to my surroundings.

In my professional universe – successful people never retire! A few pertinent thoughts that come to my mind are –

Business is an ongoing sport

An entry into the professional arena does not have a door marked exit. You are in the game, till you feel the rush of adrenaline. If the charm wanes you reinvent the sport, try other moves and tactics that infuse enthusiasm and rejuvenate yourself. The business arena is always bustling with activity and novelty. It is for you to discover the throbbing pulse of excitement.

One gets the chance to constantly reinvent oneself and stay alive and kicking. I recall the various "spur of the moment" strategies I had made in my various start-ups. The attitudinal changes, the mindset changes, the adaptability all geared towards discovering new facets of my personality.

As I moved from one start-up to another, I realized that one successful business was not the golden goose that would lay golden eggs. In fact, I could reinvent the perspective and say that I was the golden goose who could move on and create the proverbial golden eggs with more successful businesses.

Helping other entrepreneur's is a strong motivation to move ahead.

I identified a deep passion within me to help young start-up founders and entrepreneur's. Being in the business was according to me the best way of helping others set up theirs. With the business world evolving one has to be a hands-on practitioner rather than a has been and was there kinds. What held good for me at the time that I started is definitely not what would help the newbies today.

The entrepreneur has evolved from the prince on horseback who set out on his journey relying only on his physical prowess and skill to brave odds to the modern jet setting suave business mogul who now has an array of gadgets and digitalization at his disposal to traverse the territory.

Money has never been and will never be my sole motivation – it's the thrill of work that drives me!

There is no denying the fact that money is a strong motivator in my life as it is I am sure in the lives of many others, but it never was and never will be my sole motivation. I had earned well enough to absorb the inherent risks of my second innings. I had created a bubble of comfort for my family and that felt good. Beyond the comfort zone that money created, was the lure of work that was never at a standstill, ever engaging, ever absorbing. Each day brought something new that tried my skills. my abilities, made me elated, made me dejected, yet the enthusiasm and excitement that would perhaps dwindle at times was quick to be fanned back to flames of huge and meaningful activity.

Each new day posed a challenge to inspire me. It was a way of life which had grown on me and couldn't be given up. It had grown upon me like second skin. One doesn't reach the mountain top with a single success, there are several other peaks that are waiting to be explored and conquered to label your mission successful.

A career is a journey of constant growth and is an unending game.

21

Vantage Point– A Bird 's Eye View!

While I have always maintained that speed is essential for progress, I have also propagated the need to look back to see the distance covered. Looking back, I strongly believe, will always help you move forward, as contradictory as that may sound.

One of my closest and if I may say finest observations has been of the obsession of entrepreneur's with quick successes that form an integral part of their start-up dream. With that as a guiding factor, they breathlessly race ahead from one challenge to another, not permitting enough time for the dust to settle down on the previous one.

The act of pausing, reflecting and looking back have always been unfairly associated with losing momentum and pausing progress.

With wise observations on why the windshield is bigger than the rear-view mirror, one must also acknowledge that you don't need a clutter of objects in the rear-view. It has a narrower and more focused view reflecting only the important objects that you have left behind as you move ahead. The windshield with a wider vision, gives you the scope to choose from a broader array in the future.

I had reached a point in my career journey which gave me reason to look back and deliberate. With a colourful bouquet of work in the past 20 years, it was time now to sit back and inhale its' fragrance.

I envisioned the first day after I had officially shed my corporate labels and tags and moved into the start-up ocean. The barrage of criticism, the bewildered looks, the condescending looks, the pitying

looks at having kicked up my successful career, did shake me up a bit but never enough for me to give up or sink into despondency. You may well ask how I evaded that, and my answer would be through these ***shining start-up pearls of wisdom*** which I gathered and look back on in my rear-view mirror —

As a corporate leader I had not been much of a crusader for designations and fancy visiting cards, and as long as the rewards of my labour and the accompanying frills were coming in, I was comfortable just being recognized publicly as a successful leader. I would jokingly tell my secretary whenever she meticulously replenished my visiting card holder, that I always carried my visiting card on my shoulders – my face!

Once into the start-up phase I was proved completely wrong by the Director of Sales and Marketing of a reputed hotel and my business colleague, the Managing Director of a reputed company. The hospitality of the former and my meeting requests with the latter, for business sans my designation and title were pooh poohed and almost dismissed with scorn. For them, unlike me designations spelt recognition.

All my start-ups gave me a permanent designation which I would never have to surrender. I was the founder, the Director and people recognized me as one. It worked for both of us. I being more or less designation averse just had one designation by default. For the others that was who I was – the top man with a befitting designation that clearly warranted attention. I was the perfect candidate for acknowledgments in the lobby of a hotel by the Director Sales and Marketing, and my designation granted me the access past the secretaries to meet their bosses.

What emerged next in my train of thoughts was my myopic vision as I would sit in the board room of the large corporates that I worked for. As the boss of a team responsible for sales and marketing, I was a hard task master. I thought of the numerous meetings that would figure on my daily agenda as I would reveal my independent observations (and there would be plenty of them,) to the senior employees on what was wrong with their functional areas and responsibilities. On a few occasions I would even lace it with thinly veiled contempt for their decisions made and their style of working.

Fast forward to the start-up phase and I recalled how the buck stopped with me. Daily meetings formed a rather frugal part of the work agenda. The focus was more on movement and action. Correction and rectification of deeds and strategies. I and me became the predominant words as compared to you and they. I inspired commitment, and a sense of responsibility by my complete involvement.

It would be wrong to say that I wasn't completely involved with my corporate jobs, I was. It was an unparalleled, uninhibited degree of passion and loyalty that start-ups inspired which surpassed those previously felt corporate emotions. At best in my corporate role which I was delivering with whole hearted enthusiasm and dedication, I was vying for enrolment in the success stories that would be framed to decorate the corporate corridors. These would later be recounted to my successors as a part of the well-planned PR strategy of the mandatory induction programmes. They would slowly but surely breathe in the history of the great company that they would be working for. They would then don their caps with great aplomb and hope, that someday they too would figure in the future induction programme corporate success stories.

As for the start-ups. the loyalty, the involvement were all placed in a different frame.

Unlike the desire to feature in corporate lores in my jobs, in my start-ups, I was strongly motivated with a different sense of purpose – that of creating a legacy!

The next pearl from my musings was that corporate positions, tend to offer narrower roles. If you are designated a manager, you manage. If you are sales personnel, no matter how tempted you are to peep into your PR colleagues' presentation and make a few suggestions, you are confined by the shackles of your designation. Re-living my start-up days, I saw how engulfed I was by the various roles. I had to recruit and manage a team of employees, write a training manual, plan induction programmes, organize employee welfare activities, execute performance appraisals, in short be the sole member HR department. My sales and marketing role would see me designing marketing ads, creatives, flyers, making pitches and presentations, accompanying team members to client meetings, targeting prospective customers etc. My administrative duties too, were all-encompassing, right from managing the stationery requirements, to the office crockery and cutlery etc. These duties were perhaps more pronounced in the initial days of the start-ups, yet there was an inherent continuity of donning several caps, without any full stops.

Exploring your multi-faceted personality, unleashing different skills for different job roles is much more liberating and fulfilling than a strait jacketed role with the risk of monotony, limited room and scope for experimentation.

The start-up eco system is an incubator of ideas but most of the times it is bootstrapped. Corporate jobs on the contrary, come with financial backing and reserves of wealth. You may have to resort to conserving and managing finances. The aftermath of the financial struggles in start-ups I realized was worth every penny. The initial profits, the joy of achieving targets, exceeding projected sales, acquiring new projects and customers – felt nothing short of delirious joy.

The progression from less to more in start-ups comes with the coveted promise of endorsing your efforts and time and catapulting your confidence and performance to hitherto unscaled peaks of success.

People are integral to any organization and therefore having the right mix of people, with the right mindset propels an organization to success. High paying jobs lure people. Once in, making quick bucks and climbing up the corporate ladder features high on the priority list of employees. Somewhere down the line we lose sight of interaction, the exchange of ideas, the participative culture.

A start-up on the other hand is closer knit with all the employees sharing a common vision and goal for the betterment of the company and theirs too. I recalled the times when I saw the resilience, compassion, the spirit of cooperation and the humane qualities of my employees. During the loss of a family member how the group came together empathetically, how a quick lunch was arranged for an employee who had forgotten his tiffin at home, how a pregnant employee was asked almost ordered not to travel by the hired auto rickshaw and how as an alternative to this mode of commuting, a few employees formed a group for a pool car.

I recollect the times when birthdays, and wedding anniversaries were not relegated as an HR exercise to mere pop-up windows on the intranet. Instead of that common corporate practice, Ramakant's wife had woken up at the crack of dawn just to cook a delicious South Indian spread of idli, sambhar and other lip-smacking delicacies for the entire office. How the birthday boy, the center of attraction Dilip's eyes had welled up with tears while eating that had nothing to do with the spicy food that he was quick to attribute it to and would have liked us to believe. That was the satisfaction of bonding, that was the satisfaction of sharing, that was the satisfaction of caring, in a close knit start-up culture.

Human emotions shine brighter in a start-up culture. The corporate shine and glamour make the humane qualities and bonding pale by comparison!

It is wise for me to emphasize once again, that these are purely my observations and very personal. There is always room for disagreements, arguments and counter arguments.

Discord and Disruption in my opinion, have always been the precursor of progression. This is the thought that I will carry forward in my concluding chapter to talk about my future 20 years..................

22 On and beyond........

After an intense start-up studded 20 years, I was the perfect candidate for a potbellied sense of achievement, well qualified to give myself occasional pats on the back, as I looked back at my numerous successes. The strongest temptation would have been to give in to the lure of the plateau of contentment that beckoned me invitingly.

I however, belonged to the other school of thought, where life was all about momentum, life was all about speed, albeit with varying intensities, reflections and well-placed pauses. Life to me was synonymous with progress and moving on. The career landscape had unveiled its' own unique topography, which I like other individuals had traversed using either my own resources or seeking those from the external environment or combining both.

One thought that emerged very strongly and which I could see with distinct clarity in my minds' eye was that the saga of my career had not yet reached the end. My story, my journey, was still unfolding and had many more chapters to be written and re written. My retrospection and introspection of the past 20 years had only refueled and recharged me with greater vigour and energy. My start-up puzzle was filled with several pieces, each piece having its own unique contribution in completing the big picture. Some of the vital pieces were:

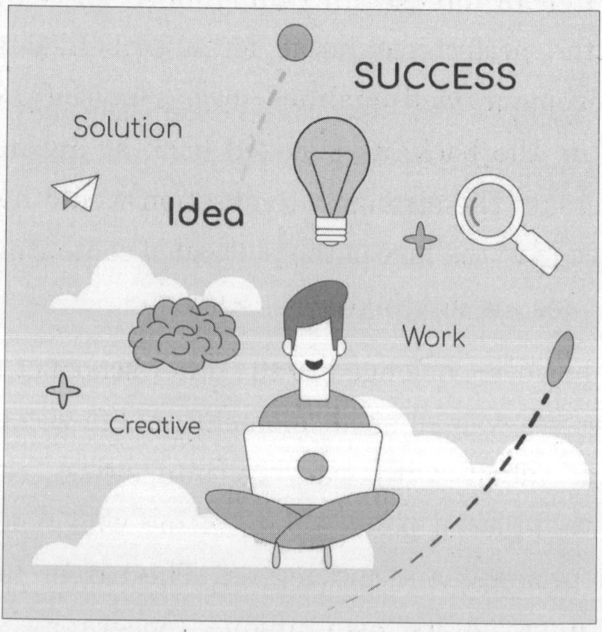

The idea – which I realized, although crucial for a start-up could not be the sole success factor. It had to be combined effectively with the others.

My juices start-up idea or the self-defense for women idea in the wellness venture, by themselves were superstars, but could not fit into the business script, to become blockbusters.

Leadership – This definitely has to be strong. It has to create a participative culture. A skilled and involved leader can transform even a weak idea into a strong one.

My partners in the Edu-Tech start-up who were risk averse and played condescending roles, never really did get down to the brass tacks and failed to inspire the team.

The team – The people factor is a major success driver in start-ups. Hire the right people and watch the start-up zoom, hire the wrong people and see the death of even the best ideas.

I learnt this the hard way. After having hired top people with top labelled qualifications that translated into top egos, I settled for people with top qualifications who traded the labels with their passion which worked miracles for the company.

Capital – There is no denying the importance of working capital. Relying on personal or familial investments is pretty much the done thing. Opening a line of credit is also an option. What must be watched with a hawk's eye is frugality in spending, guarding against splurging without a plan or an objective. One wrong move is enough to spell the start-up doom.

In my failed start-up, this was one of the harsh lessons I learnt.

Keeping an exit plan handy – the oxymoronic attachment with detachment – You've done it all, given your life, sweat and blood and if it is not working out then you must have the discerning ability to know when it's time to exit. Loss making companies as well as profitable companies need an exit strategy. When you feel you have given your last ounce of wisdom, expertise and hard work to drive a company either to the top or amongst the first few, it's once again time to exit. Selling off your equity, making a profit and moving on elsewhere to shower your expertise and build another success story should be the strategy.

I had the prudence and discretion to exit my failed start-ups in time and sell off my equity in the profitable ones just in time too.

The planning, execution and timing – the plan is another integral part of a start-up success, yet it must include much more than just your core idea. Your objectives, your targets, your methods of operation and a lot more. The more fine-tuned your plan is, the higher chances of success you have. A great plan with a botched-up execution spells disaster. A solid plan backed by good execution give you a strong foundation. Timing is another crucial factor that is keyed into successes. The perfect launch timing, the introduction or reintroduction of an idea, product or service is the clincher.

In the document storage company, we had struck when the iron was hot and come up with new strategies and planned for our success.

Crisis preparedness, PR, marketing and growth – Dealing with crisis and trying situations is a norm of business life, hence preparedness is the key. PR and Marketing are equally essential. Having a good product but not reaching out to potential clients is a nonstarter in any case, so create good PR and marketing visibility. In a social media-controlled world where the consumer can be reached in fractions of seconds, I would be happy to dispel the myth of "don't judge a book by its cover." Branding and visual appeal is the first breakthrough you make in a customer's mind and attention span. If your product and service is good and offers what it promises, success will eventually follow.

In the wellness venture, we had done all of this formally and informally that translated into huge success for us.

Growth –This is slippery territory and needs to be treated with kids gloves. If you grow too fast, you will end up stretching yourself too thin, on the other hand growing slowly will push you back a thousand years. Striking a balance and treating growth with a well-planned strategy is what you need.

In all my successful ventures I had a sharp eye on this.

There is a profound wisdom in the saying "The old order changeth, yielding place to new" or quite simply put, "out with the old, in with the new."

This would be the beacon of light shining brightly on my professional life for the next 20 years...

As a seasoned professional, a priceless realization dawned upon me -

Moving forward would not include copying successful blueprints of the past!

Yet it would definitely include careful evaluation of what went into the successes and if those components could be utilized in the modern times with a few tweaks. It would also include lessons learnt from the past. The mistakes, the failures et al.

The writing on the wall was loud and clear – adapt or perish!

For the modern entrepreneur's this could well be cited as the maxim for all businesses. The COVID-19 pandemic has been one of our greatest teachers. It has taught all of us the need for change and adaptability. The WFH (Work from Home) culture has unveiled aspects of work and work styles that were hitherto unthought of. It is almost as if we have peeled off our earlier mindset and accepted a fresh new perspective of business.

Even without a COVID ridden world, technology and business practices had evolved. The business strategies that I had adopted for my earlier successes would definitely not hold true for my future ones because I had come to terms with "change is the only constant."

As I went about conducting my new set of meetings, planning my new ventures, I adopted the mindset of the new age entrepreneur's. The modern entrepreneur has a strong focus on creating technology driven solutions, with AI ruling the roost. One of my ongoing ventures is with a company that is global AI driven company. I have adopted digitalization in all my new ventures. Innovation and cutting age technology are the backbone of another start-up of mine.

The new trend shows the shift of the investor community both angel and venture capitalists towards funding and mentoring creative and innovative ventures. The accent is more on associating with a novel idea than just making a profit.

I am enthused to inform you that I am associated with at least 4 start-ups today that can all be bracketed under the "think our of the box" companies. Modern technology has unfurled a wide choice for the new age entrepreneur -AI, 5G, IOT, machine learning, or blockchain. The start-ups today are harnessing disruption. New trends and technologies are replacing the older norms and the tried and tested ways of doing things.

With the new start-up ecosystem growing at an incredible pace as a founder of my new start-ups have seized the opportunity to disrupt and flourish. The plan in my head has the clear objective of being in the spotlight for start-ups with the most ground breaking ideas. As for success, an optimistic me, sees it close at my heels.

My career houses the inseparable trilogy of yesterday, today and tomorrow. Yesterday was rife with enthusiasm, to prove to myself and to the world that I could achieve what I had set out for, today was all about the passion of working, seizing opportunities and moving from one success to another. Tomorrow is filled with hope and unexplored potential and possibilities.

I am once again, hands-on, doing what I love doing the most – start-ups! My mixed bag of exciting new ventures encompasses the sports tech area, conversational AI, Digital Ad agency and a neuromarketing start-up. I have established Innovation Clubs in schools as well as an Edu-Tech start-up.

I have now donned the mantle of a mentor, and am enjoying my new role of guiding young and budding entrepreneur's pro bono. I strongly believe in the power of young entrepreneur's to transform the start-up landscape. The passionate professional in me helps me in identifying the young entrepreneur's and catching them young, and mentoring them to perfection. My rational side ruled by my business acumen directs me to hold an equity in their ventures.

Their youth and enthusiasm is contagious and rubs off on me as well.

I feel the same enthusiasm that I felt 20 years ago when I set foot on the unexplored territory of start-ups. I look to the heavens above with a silent and fervent prayer to kccp this spark alive for another 20 years.

Nothing has changed and nothing will is what I say to reassure myself as I start my car to drive down to work.

As if in affirmation of my thoughts the radio plays "Yesterday once more!"

I metamorphose into the dreamy eyed young entrepreneur once again and sing along – "all my best memories come back clearly to me."

I then go ahead to add my own meaningful lyrics, that echo my mood and sentiments –

"Let's create yesterday once more..."